# TRUE CRIME SLEEP STORIES

VOLUME 2

KELLI BRINK

BEYOND
THE FRAY PUBLISHING

Published by Beyond The Fray Publishing



ISBN 13: 979-8-89234-126-4

Beyond The Fray Publishing,
a division of Beyond The Fray, LLC
San Diego, CA

# DEDICATION

*To the remarkable men who have profoundly shaped my life—my heart overflows with gratitude for your unwavering support and love.*

*To my late father, Larry, whose immense pride in me lit a fire within. You taught me resilience, creativity, and the value of hard work. You taught me to be strong and to "never go to bed angry". Though you're not physically here to share in my achievements, I feel your presence with every step I take, and I miss you ever-so-much. I cherish our memories and wish we could still chat over a whiskey. I love you, Dad.*

*To my brother, John, my second father figure, who stepped in with strength and guidance. Thank you for sharing your wisdom, teaching me about the world beyond my doorstep, about strength and survival, and nurturing my adventurous spirit. Your support is a cherished gift.*

*To Patrick, "The Captain," my dear supportive friend, who lifts me up with endless encouragement and pushes me to be my best every day. Your belief in me has been a guiding light through every challenge. Your ideas and enthusiasm have been a blessing.*

*To Chris, my friend and coparent, who has always encouraged my strengths and ambitions. You are one of the best humans I know. Your unwavering support has been a foundation I deeply appreciate. I simply couldn't do any of this without you.*

*In a world where the positive influence of men so often goes uncelebrated, I find myself fortunate beyond words to be surrounded by remarkable male role models who have shaped my life in countless ways. While the stories within these pages may showcase the darker side of humanity, I am constantly reminded by the incredible men around me that true masculinity is far from toxic. Your support, strength, and guidance have been my foundation, inspiring me to reach for my best self every day. Thank you for being the anchors in my life.*

# CONTENTS

# INTRODUCTION

Welcome to *True Crime Sleep Stories, Volume 2*—a chilling continuation of our first book, where shadowy mysteries and spine-tingling tales come alive. Prepare to be ensnared by a fresh collection of stories that weave through the darkest corners of history and right up to our own doorsteps. Here, within the confines of your own safe haven, you can explore the eerie and unsettling threads of human nature that have baffled, shocked, and intrigued for centuries.

These stories are designed to transport you through time, starting with the ghastly unsolved murders of the 1800s. Picture the gaslit streets and fog-covered alleys, where whispers of unspeakable deeds carried on the wind haunt the night. These mysteries, never fully unraveled, continue to captivate those who dare to ponder what truly may have transpired in those shadowed corners.

Our narrative then winds its way to more recent times, examining perplexing crimes that defy logic and challenge our understanding of human morality and justice. Each tale is meticulously crafted to entertain and provoke thought, ensuring that each page turn uncovers more than just another story—it's a puzzle waiting to be pieced together.

But it doesn't end with the tangible. Some stories venture into the realm of residual hauntings, where the energy of past wrongs lingers, leaving ghostly imprints on the very air we breathe. Imagine places where the atmosphere is thick with the presence of those who once lived and tragically perished, their stories etched into the walls as a spectral echo of history.

Not every narrative within these pages is a crime in the conventional sense. Some hover between fact and fiction, skimming the edges of possible hoaxes or legends passed down through generations. Yet every story complements the others, collectively forming a tapestry of suspense that ensures you'll be drifting off with a heightened sense of awareness—even if only for a moment.

Dive into this volume and allow its haunting allure to wrap around you like a dark, comforting blanket. Whether you're a steadfast true crime enthusiast, a lover of enigmatic mysteries, or a history buff with a penchant for the past's more sinister side, these stories promise to ignite your imagination and keep you pondering long after the lights go out.

As you settle into the cozy corner of your favorite room, let the glow of your reading lamp draw you closer into the realm of mystery. With each page, dim the lights and allow the shadows to stretch, inviting a hushed stillness that perfectly sets the scene for a journey through chilling tales.

# INTRODUCTION

Wrapped in a plush blanket and cradling a warm cup of tea, get ready to be whisked away into a world where the eerie and unknown beckon in whispers. Let go of the day's stress and surrender to these relaxing yet thrilling tales of terror—a sanctuary of suspense awaits.

# CHAPTER ONE

## PEARL BRYAN AND HER MISSING HEAD

In the chilling winter of 1896, the quiet town of Greencastle, Indiana, was rocked by an event so unsettling that it still reverberates through the annals of true crime history. Pearl Bryan, a vibrant 22-year-old who spent her Sundays teaching at the local church, vanished under mysterious circumstances. She was last seen setting off on what her family believed was a mundane trip to visit a friend in Indianapolis. What they didn't know was that Pearl carried a secret — she was five months pregnant.

Her disappearance soon spiraled into a tale of horror that would grip the nation. Less than a week after her departure, a grisly discovery was made over 150 miles away in Fort Thomas, Kentucky. Pearl's decapitated body was found, with her head severed just below the fifth vertebra. Despite exhaustive searches, her head was never recovered, casting an enduring shadow of mystery over her tragic fate.

Pearl's story began to take shape in the spring of 1895 when she met Scott Jackson, a man whose charm masked a sinister intent. Unbeknownst to her family, Pearl had fallen pregnant by Jackson, who lured her to Cincinnati, Ohio, under the pretense of arranging an abortion. However, instead of offering her the assistance she desperately sought, Jackson orchestrated her murder, forever sealing Pearl's fate in one of the most sensational crimes Northern Kentucky had ever witnessed.

Despite the passage of time, Pearl Bryan's story refuses to be forgotten. Her brutal murder and the enigma of her missing head continue to captivate true crime enthusiasts and historians alike. Some even say her restless spirit haunts Bobby Mackey's Music World in Wilder, Kentucky, a testament to a life tragically cut short and a mystery that remains unsolved.

---

Pearl Bryan emerged into the world as the youngest of the twelve children born to the esteemed Alexander S. Bryan and his wife, Susan Jane. In the rural heart of Greencastle, Indiana, where her father was a pillar of the farming community, Pearl's life unfolded with the promise and potential characteristic of a small-town dream. She proudly completed her education at Greencastle High School in 1892, earning a reputation for her intelligence and dedication.

Brimming with youthful optimism and determination, Pearl embarked on a new chapter, dedicating herself to teaching Sunday school—a testament to her nurturing spirit and commitment to her community. However, the fateful decision she made on January 28, 1896, would cast a long shadow over her promising life. Leaving her family's home under the guise of visiting a friend in Indianapolis, Pearl unknowingly set in motion a series of events that would lead to her demise.

Pearl's life took a complicated turn when she entered a romantic relationship with Scott Jackson, a promising 28-year-old dental student at the Ohio College of Dental Surgery. Their secret affair resulted in Pearl's pregnancy, a revelation that would stir the conservative waters of her close-knit community.

Determined to avert scandal, Pearl's cousin, Will Wood, reached out to Jackson, pleading for a solution to protect the family's honor. Jackson, with unsettling confidence, assured Wood that he could "fix her," a sinister promise documented in the archives of the Enquirer.

The correspondence between Jackson and his accomplice, Alonzo Walling, a 20-year-old fellow student and roommate, revealed a chilling conspiracy. Initially, Walling was led to believe that they were to perform a secret abortion. However, as the plan unfurled, it became clear that Jackson harbored a darker intention—to poison Pearl and stage her death as a tragic suicide.

The truth of their vile plot was exposed through the autopsy findings, which revealed a brutal injection of prussic acid as the cause of Pearl's untimely demise. Whether this lethal dose was meant to terminate her pregnancy - or to silence her forever - remains an unresolved mystery, adding yet another layer of intrigue and horror to this grim tale.

## The Gruesome Discovery

On a chilling, fog-laden morning in February of 1896, a 17-year-old farmhand named Johnny Hewling made a discovery that would shock the small town of Fort Thomas, Kentucky. Cutting across the field near the corner of Highland Avenue and Alexandria Pike—a plot owned by his employer, Colonel John Lock—Johnny stumbled upon the lifeless body of a woman.

At first glance, he wasn't sure if the woman was dead or merely intoxicated, as the area was known for its discreet encounters between soldiers and local women. "Many women came here with soldiers for secret meetings," Johnny later recounted. "Finding someone drunk wasn't unusual."

Once alerted to the situation, Colonel Lock summoned a deputy sheriff to investigate. Among those who arrived at the scene was Coroner Bob Tingley. What they found was beyond anyone's darkest imaginations—a pool of blood suggested a violent struggle had taken place, and when Tingley turned the body over, the grim truth was revealed. The woman had been decapitated.

Despite a thorough search of the surrounding area, the woman's head was nowhere to be found. Bloodhounds followed a scent trail to the Covington Reservoir, but even after it was drained, the search yielded no results. The body was taken to Newport for an autopsy, revealing the woman was five months pregnant and had cocaine in her stomach—a possible indication of her killer's earlier intentions.

Identification of the body was achieved through a meticulous trace of her custom-made shoes from Greencastle, Indiana. The manufacturer's number led authorities to a shoe store and then to Pearl Bryan's family.

**Suspects and Convictions**

In a case that captured national attention and became the talk of the era, two promising dental students at the Ohio College of Dental Surgery found their futures irrevocably altered. Scott Jackson, a confident young man with a mind as sharp as his scalpel, was arrested for the brutal murder of Pearl Bryan. His conviction soon implicated his roommate, Alonzo M. Walling, an enigmatic character whose brooding demeanor masked a pliant nature, easily swayed by Jackson's persuasive charisma.

Their trials unveiled a dark narrative of betrayal and deception. Jackson, it seemed, had been entangled in a romance with Bryan for several months. Evidence suggested that on January 31, 1896, Jackson and Walling had lured Bryan to a Cincinnati saloon, slipping cocaine into her drink before ending her life later that night. The presence of cocaine in Bryan's system, confirmed through forensic analysis, painted a damning picture of premeditation.

The mystery deepened with the macabre absence of Bryan's head, a grim detail that stoked public fascination and horror. Jackson and Walling offered conflicting accounts, suggesting it could be anywhere from the murky depths of the Ohio River to the sandy stretches of Dayton, Kentucky. Desperate searches around these locales yielded nothing, leading many, including former detective Cal Crim, to speculate that the head met its fiery demise in the furnace of their dental college—a theory that remains unproven to this day.

Jackson's trial commenced on April 21 and concluded on May 14, 1896, with Walling's following shortly after, from May 26 to June 18. Both were found guilty of first-degree murder, their fates sealed with a sentence to hang on March 20, 1897. The execution was a public spectacle of grim efficiency, marred by the botched initial drop that left both men gasping for life in front of a transfixed audience.

This case, widely covered by the press, sparked a nationwide frenzy. Citizens flocked to the crime scene, snatching souvenirs, while the local economy capitalized on the tragedy with Pearl Bryan-themed merchandise. The trials were described as "theatrical," dubbed "the trial of the century" by local papers.

Amid the turmoil, Jackson and Walling's final days were marked by fear of vigilante justice. Even during a jailbreak at Newport jail, the duo remained in their cells, protected by heavy police presence against possible lynching. Their execution was a cautious affair, carefully orchestrated despite the palpable tension and the looming threat of mob violence.

Jackson, a man of complex background, stood at the gallows with a defiant air, revealing nothing of Bryan's missing head, despite the promise of clemency for Walling if he confessed. His silence sealed both their fates, and they faced their end with Jackson maintaining his innocence, casting himself as a victim of circumstance rather than a perpetrator of violence.

Walling, less composed, trembled as he faced his doom, his final words a desperate plea of innocence. Yet, despite their claims, the execution proceeded, and the gallows behind the Newport Campbell County Courthouse claimed its last victims, etching their story into true crime history.

The aftermath of this sensational case left a lasting legacy, immortalizing Bryan's tragic end and the unanswered questions that still haunt those who dig into this unsettling chapter of American history. In Greencastle, Indiana, Pearl Bryan's story remains alive in a hauntingly poignant tradition. Visitors to her grave often leave pennies on her tombstone, a symbolic gesture hoping to reunite her with her missing head on resurrection day.

Pearl's legacy, as tragic as it is enduring, finds resonance in various cultural expressions. Her gruesome murder inspired numerous folk songs during the 1910s and 1920s, capturing the macabre fascination of the era. American country singer Vernon Dalhart was the first to immortalize her story in a song recorded in 1926. This was followed by Bradley Kincaid's rendition in 1927, aptly titled "Pearl Bryan." Folk musicians like Dick Burnett and Leonard Rutherford also lent their voices to this chilling narrative, ensuring Pearl's story transcended oral folklore.

Fast-forward to 2001, when the melody of Pearl's tale reverberated through the strings of The Crooked Jades, a San Francisco-based folklore band. Their song echoed the dark corridors of history, reminding listeners of the enduring mystery. Pearl's story has also captivated the paranormal world; an episode of Ghost Adventures dissected the eerie claims of hauntings at Bobby Mackey's Music World, where Bryan's spirit is rumored to linger.

Her tale has become a staple for many paranormal shows, cementing her presence in the supernatural realm.

The question that has haunted imaginations for decades remains unanswered—where is Pearl Bryan's head? Speculation abounds, with some suggesting that it was sold to medical schools, which, during the late 1800s, accepted body parts without question. Others believe it was discarded in an old well recently uncovered in the basement of Bobby Mackey's Music World.

The murder of Pearl Bryan is undeniably tragic, filled with layers of deception and betrayal. While Jackson's guilt seems certain, Walling's involvement remains cloaked in ambiguity—did he merely aid in concealing the crime, or was he complicit from the start? The cold detachment with which Jackson committed such heinous acts, including the murder of an unborn child, raises disturbing questions about his capacity for cruelty. His willingness to sacrifice Walling to the gallows alongside him offers a chilling insight into his character.

Ultimately, the full truth may remain forever out of reach, but Pearl's legacy endures. Her story is a testament to the enduring power of human intrigue and the unrelenting quest for justice—a narrative that invites us to ponder the mysteries that lie unsolved.

# CHAPTER TWO

## THE UNFATHOMABLE DARKNESS OF ALBERT FISH

In the shadowy corners of American crime, few figures evoke as much dread and bewilderment as Hamilton Howard "Albert" Fish. Born on May 19, 1870, Fish's life would unfold to paint a sinister tapestry of murder, cannibalism, and depravity that defies comprehension. Known by a plethora of chilling monikers—The Gray Man, The Werewolf of Wysteria, The Brooklyn Vampire, The Moon Maniac, and The Boogey Man—Fish's reign of terror spanned the mid-1920s, leaving an indelible mark on the nation.

Fish's heinous acts included at least three confirmed child murders between July 1924 and June 1928. Yet, his confessions alluded to a far more extensive and darker repertoire, hinting at a possible 100 victims—a statement whose veracity remains shrouded in uncertainty. Arrested on December 13, 1934, Fish faced justice for the heinous kidnapping and murder of young Grace Budd. In what became a highly publicized trial, he was convicted and subsequently executed by electric chair on January 16, 1936, at the age of 65.

## A Troubled Beginning

Albert Fish's early years foreshadowed the chaos and malevolence that characterized his later life. Born in Washington, D.C., to Randall Fish, a man 43 years his mother's senior, and Ellen Francis Howell, Albert was the youngest of four children.

The Fish family was deeply entangled with mental illness. His uncle and several siblings were plagued by various psychological disorders, a familial curse that seemed to extend to Fish himself. After his father's sudden death from a heart attack, young Albert found himself thrust into the harsh environment of Saint John's Orphanage, where he endured - and disturbingly embraced - frequent beatings.

## Descent into Depravity

Freed from the orphanage's clutches by his mother in 1880, Fish's life took a darker turn in 1882 when, at just 12 years old, he began a relationship with a telegraph boy. This association introduced him to disturbing practices, including the consumption of human waste, setting Fish on a path of deviant behavior. He became a familiar face at public baths, fixated on watching other boys undress—a harbinger of the predatory tendencies that would later define his criminal career.

Albert Fish's infamy was further fueled by his penchant for writing obscene letters to women, sourced from personal ads and matrimonial agencies. These letters, laced with lewdness and menace, provided a glimpse into the warped psyche of a man who thrived on fear and inflicted pain.

As we explore the harrowing chapters of Fish's life and crimes, we unravel the complexities of a man whose malevolence seemed boundless. In understanding Fish, we confront the chilling reality of human darkness at its most extreme.

## The Grim Descent of Albert Fish

In the bustling heart of New York City around 1890, a young Albert Fish arrived, wide-eyed and eager to make his mark. At just twenty years old, the city offered Fish more than he could have imagined—a place where shadows lingered in every corner and secrets whispered through the alleys. It was in this labyrinth of anonymity that Fish began a chilling chapter of his life, seeking out the vulnerable and indulging in dark desires that would haunt him for decades.

Fish's early years in New York were marked by disturbing behavior. He engaged in male prostitution and preyed upon young boys, most under the tender age of six, leaving a trail of trauma in his wake. By 1898, Fish's life took a seemingly normal turn when his mother arranged a marriage to Anna Mary Hoffman, nine years his junior. Together, they had six children—Albert, Anna, Gertrude, Eugene, John, and Henry. Yet, beneath this facade of domesticity lay Fish's compulsion for criminality. In 1903, he found himself behind bars at Sing Sing Prison, convicted of grand larceny.

For his children, life seemed ordinary until 1917, when the family unit shattered. Fish's wife abandoned him for another man, leaving Fish grappling with reality and the task of raising their children alone. Disturbingly, it was during this tumultuous time that his children noted Fish's penchant for bizarre "games." One particularly chilling activity involved them paddling their father with a nail-studded paddle until blood flowed—a testament to Fish's twisted desires. His self-inflicted punishments grew increasingly grotesque, embedding needles into his flesh and setting wool aflame inside his body.

After his wife's departure, Fish's correspondence with women revealed another layer of his depravity. He wrote letters detailing horrific sexual fantasies, though none of these women responded to his macabre proposals. With no partner to fulfill his desires, Fish traveled extensively, painting houses across various states. Some believe his choice of location was strategic, targeting areas with large African American populations, under the assumption that their disappearances would provoke less attention.

In 1910, Fish's depravity reached new depths when he met Thomas Bedden in Delaware. Their relationship culminated in a horrific two-week ordeal of torture. Fish's sadistic tendencies manifested in a nightmarish scene, culminating in the mutilation of Bedden's body—a memory Fish recounted with chilling detachment.

What began as an unsettling alliance quickly spiraled into a nightmarish descent, shrouded in the murky waters of sadomasochism. The dynamics of their relationship were ambiguous at best, with Bedden's potential cognitive impairments casting shadows over the question of consent.

After a brief ten-day period, Fish transported Bedden to an isolated farmhouse, a setting that would become the backdrop for two weeks of unimaginable torment. Fish's acts of cruelty escalated to a horrifying climax when he bound Bedden and severed half of his penis. The chilling memory of Bedden's screams and the haunting gaze he cast upon Fish was something the perpetrator would later recall vividly, a grim testament to the horror of that moment.

Fish's original plan was even more macabre; he intended to end Bedden's life, dismember his body, and take the remains home as grotesque trophies. However, the oppressive heat of the season posed a risk of attracting unwanted attention, forcing Fish to abandon his grisly intentions.

In a bizarre twist of care mixed with cruelty, Fish attempted a rudimentary treatment, pouring peroxide over the wound and wrapping it with a Vaseline-soaked handkerchief. He left Bedden with a $10 bill, a final, twisted gesture of farewell, before kissing him goodbye. Boarding the first train he could find, Fish fled the scene, never once looking back or seeking to discover Bedden's fate. The incident became another dark chapter in Fish's life.

The unraveling of Fish's psyche continued as he experienced vivid auditory hallucinations and engaged in relentless self-harm. He wrapped himself in carpets and claimed to follow divine instructions. X-rays later revealed a grotesque collection of needles imbedded within his body, physical evidence of the man's tormented mind.

While his children bore witness to his peculiar behaviors, Fish never directed his violence towards them. Yet, he drew them into his world, encouraging their participation in his self-flagellation rituals. The boundaries between pain and pleasure blurred as Fish descended further into madness.

Albert Fish's early adulthood paints the portrait of a man whose life was anything but ordinary. His story stands as a chilling tale of how deeply one can descend into darkness.

## Darkness Falls

In the shadowy alleys of Georgetown around 1919, Albert Fish's sinister proclivities began to surface with chilling intensity. His first known attack was on a vulnerable young boy with intellectual disabilities. Fish, guided by his twisted rationale, targeted those he deemed "invisible" to society—often selecting victims who were either mentally disabled or African-American, believing that their disappearances would go unnoticed.

Fish's depravity knew no bounds. He sometimes paid boys to lure other children into his grasp, ensnaring his victims with promises that belied his gruesome intentions. Once captured, these innocent souls faced Fish's self-proclaimed "implements of Hell": a meat cleaver, a butcher knife, and a small handsaw—tools of torture and death that became synonymous with his reign of terror.

On the quiet afternoon of July 11, 1924, in Staten Island, eight-year-old Beatrice Kiel was playing alone on her family's farm. Fish approached her with a cynical facade of kindness, offering money to help him search for rhubarb. Fortunately, Beatrice's mother sensed danger and intervened just in time, driving Fish away. Undeterred, Fish returned later that night, seeking refuge in their barn. It was here that Beatrice's father discovered him, forcing the intruder to flee once more.

Fish's mental state continued to deteriorate. By 1924, at 54 years old and suffering from psychosis, he claimed divine voices commanded him to commit unspeakable acts of torture and mutilation against children.

One day, while contemplating his next move, he sought out a ten-year-old boy he had previously molested—Cyril Quinn. Fish approached Cyril and his friend as they played box ball, offering them lunch. Once inside Fish's apartment, the young boys inadvertently uncovered his arsenal of horror hidden beneath the mattress. Terrified by the sight, they fled, unknowingly escaping a horrendous fate.

Meanwhile, Fish's personal life mirrored the chaos within him. Despite already being married, he wed Estella Wilcox on February 6, 1930, in Waterloo, New York. This union swiftly disintegrated, ending in divorce after just one week. His behavior continued to spiral out of control, leading to a series of arrests, including one for sending an obscene letter to a woman responding to a maid advertisement. These repeated brushes with the law eventually landed Fish in Bellevue Hospital for psychiatric observation, where experts attempted to understand the mind of this man who eluded moral and legal constraints alike.

This period of Fish's life reveals the depth of his depravity—a decade-long descent into darkness, marked by a profound disconnect from reality and a relentless pursuit of malevolent desires.

## The Murder of Grace Budd

The chilling events surrounding the murder of young Grace Budd began on a seemingly ordinary day in May 1928. Albert Fish was perusing the classifieds in the Sunday edition of the New York World. One advertisement caught his attention—a young man named Edward Budd was seeking employment in the countryside. Fish, then 58 years old, saw an opportunity not just for employment, but for something far more sinister.

On May 28, Fish visited the Budd family in Manhattan, posing as "Frank Howard," a farmer from Farmingdale, New York. His story was convincing, and he promised to hire Edward and his friend, weaving a tale that would soon turn dark. Though Fish's initial plan involved Edward, it was the presence of Edward's younger sister, 10-year-old Grace, that shifted his malevolent intentions.

Fish concocted a story about attending a niece's birthday party, persuading Delia Bridget Flanagan and Albert Francis Budd Sr., Grace's unsuspecting parents, to allow her to accompany him. Trustingly, they agreed, unwittingly sending Grace into the clutches of a monster. Fish led her to a house he had selected in East Irvington, New York—Wisteria Cottage. It was there that the unimaginable occurred.

In the isolation of that house, Fish carried out his horrific plans. He strangled Grace to death, then gruesomely dismembered her body. Over the following days, Fish engaged in acts of cannibalism, leaving behind a haunting legacy of horror and despair.

The investigation into Grace's disappearance initially led to Charles Edward Pope, a superintendent who was wrongfully accused and spent over three months in jail before being found not guilty. The true perpetrator, Albert Fish, remained free for several more years.

**Letter to the mother of Grace Budd**

It wasn't until November 1934 that the truth began to unravel. An anonymous letter arrived at the Budd household, its contents revealing the disturbing narrative of Grace's fate. Grace's mother, unable to read, had her son decipher the letter—a brutal recounting of events penned by Fish himself.

The letter began with an unsettling story about cannibalism during a famine in China, a tale meant to rationalize Fish's own dark cravings. The chilling confession detailed Fish's actions on the day he took Grace, his calculated deceit, and the appalling acts that followed.

*My dear Mrs. Budd,*

*In 1894 a friend of mine shipped as a deck hand on the Steamer Tacoma, Capt. John Davis. They sailed from San Francisco for Hong Kong China. On arriving there he and two others went ashore and got drunk. When they returned the boat was gone.*

*At that time there was famine in China. Meat of any kind was from $1 to 3 Dollars a pound. So great was the suffering among the very poor that* all children under 12 were sold for food in order to keep others from starving. A boy or girl under 14 was not safe in the street. You could go in any shop and ask for steak—chops—or stew meat. Part of the naked body of a boy or girl would be brought out and just what you wanted cut from it. A boy or girls behind which is the sweetest part of the body and sold as veal cutlet brought the highest price.

John staid [sic] there so long he acquired a taste for human flesh. On his return to N.Y., he stole two boys one 7 one 11. Took them to his home stripped them naked tied them in a closet. Then burned everything they had on. Several times every day and night he spanked them—tortured them—to make their meat good and tender.

First he killed the 11 year old boy, because he had the fattest ass and of course the most meat on it. Every part of his body was Cooked and eaten except the head—bones and guts. He was Roasted in the oven (all of his ass), boiled, broiled, fried and stewed. The little boy was next, went the same way. At that time, I was living at 409 E 100 St., near—right side. He told me so often how good Human flesh was I made up my mind to taste it.

On Sunday June the 3—1928 I called on you at 406 W 15 St. Brought you pot cheese—straw-

*berries. We had lunch. Grace sat in my lap and kissed me. I made up my mind to eat her.*

*On the pretense of taking her to a party. You said Yes she could go. I took her to an empty house in Westchester I had already picked out. When we got there, I told her to remain outside. She picked wildflowers. I went upstairs and stripped all my clothes off. I knew if I did not I would get her blood on them.*

*When all was ready I went to the window and called her. Then I hid in a closet until she was in the room. When she saw me all naked she began to cry and tried to run down the stairs. I grabbed her and she said she would tell her mamma.*

*First I stripped her naked. How she did kick —bite and scratch. I choked her to death, then cut her in small pieces so I could take my meat to my rooms. Cook and eat it. How sweet and tender her little ass was roasted in the oven. It took me 9 days to eat her entire body. I did not fuck her tho I could of had I wished. She died a virgin.*

The letter spun a tale involving "Capt. Davis" and a famine in distant Hong Kong—a narrative that investigators struggled to substantiate. However, when it came to the grim details surrounding the murder of young Grace Budd, the letter's accuracy was unnervingly precise.

The description of Grace's abduction and the subsequent events proved to align disturbingly well with the known facts of the case. Yet, the ultimate horror lay in the unverified claim that Fish had resorted to cannibalism, consuming parts of the innocent child's body. This assertion, while never conclusively proven, cast a sinister shadow over an already horrific crime, leaving a lingering question that would forever unsettle the minds of those who dared to traverse the dark corridors of this chilling narrative.

**Capture**

In New York City, a seemingly innocuous letter arrived that would unravel a chilling mystery. The envelope bore a unique hexagonal emblem embossed with the letters "N.Y.P.C.B.A."—the insignia of the New York Private Chauffeur's Benevolent Association. What connected this stationery to a gruesome crime was a twist of fate.

A janitor who once worked for the association casually mentioned to the police that he had taken some of the stationery home. However, he had left it behind at his previous lodging, a rooming house at 200 East 52nd Street, when he relocated. This small detail turned out to be a pivotal clue.

The landlady of the rooming house recalled a tenant named Albert Fish, who had checked out just days earlier. She mentioned that Fish's son regularly sent him money, and Fish had instructed her to hold onto his next check.

Detective William King, the investigator leading the case, decided to stake out the rooming house. His patience was rewarded when Fish eventually returned. Without raising suspicion, Fish agreed to accompany King to police headquarters for questioning. However, once there, Fish revealed a hidden razor blade, his intentions unclear but certainly sinister. Detective King swiftly disarmed him, ensuring Fish would be brought to justice.

In a shocking confession, Fish did not hesitate to admit to the murder of young Grace Budd. He revealed that his original plan was to kill her brother, Edward. Disturbingly, Fish claimed that the thought of raping Grace "never even entered [his] head." Yet, in a grotesque revelation to his attorney, Fish admitted that while strangling the child, he experienced two involuntary ejaculations. This horrific detail was strategically used in court to suggest a sexually motivated kidnapping, conveniently sidestepping the more repulsive truth of cannibalism.

### Additional Fish Crimes: The Grisly Tale of Francis McDonnell

It was a warm evening on July 14, 1924, when the peaceful community of Port Richmond, Staten Island, was shattered by the disappearance of young Francis McDonnell. The 9-year-old had been playing catch with friends, a simple pastime that soon turned into tragedy. When Francis failed to return home, alarm spread through the neighborhood, prompting a frantic search.

The following day, the horror was unveiled. Francis's lifeless body was discovered hanging from a tree in a wooded area near his residence. He had been subjected to unspeakable violence—sexually assaulted, strangled with his suspenders, and brutally mutilated. The autopsy revealed gruesome lacerations across his legs and abdomen, with his left hamstring nearly stripped bare of flesh.

Initially, there seemed no clear suspect. But whispers of a shadowy figure emerged. Friends of Francis recounted seeing the boy with an elderly man sporting a gray mustache. One neighbor corroborated their account, having observed the duo walking into the nearby woods.

Francis's mother, Anna, provided an eerie description of the stranger. She recalled seeing an old man with thick gray hair and a drooping gray mustache who had shuffled down the street, mumbling incoherently while gesturing oddly with his hands. It was this haunting description that gave rise to the moniker "The Grey Man."

Despite the police's efforts, the case went cold until it was rekindled by the murder of Grace Budd. Eyewitnesses, including a local farmer, recognized Albert Fish as the strange figure seen on the day of Francis's disappearance. Though Fish initially denied involvement, he eventually confessed to the murder after his trial for Grace Budd's murder concluded. The New York Daily Mirror would later label Fish as "the most vicious child-slayer in criminal history."

**The Disappearance of Billy Gaffney**

Fast forward to February 11, 1927, in Brooklyn, where the atmosphere was thick with mystery and fear. Three-year-old Billy Beaton and his older brother had been playing in their apartment hallway with four-year-old Billy Gaffney. When the older brother briefly returned to their apartment, both younger boys vanished. Billy Beaton was later found on the roof, but there was no sign of Billy Gaffney.

When questioned, Billy Beaton offered a chilling response, "The bogeyman took him." Initially, suspicion fell upon serial killer Peter Kudzinowski, but the case took a chilling turn when Joseph Meehan, a trolley motorman, identified Fish from a newspaper photo. Meehan vividly recalled an old man attempting to calm a distressed little boy on a trolley—believed to be Gaffney. The boy, missing his jacket and crying for his mother, was dragged off the vehicle by the man.

Police discovered that Fish had been working as a house painter in Brooklyn, just a short distance from where Gaffney disappeared. Despite her grief, Elizabeth Gaffney, Billy's mother, confronted Fish in Sing Sing Prison, yet Fish refused to divulge any details about her son's fate.

However, Fish later composed a letter to his attorney, describing in harrowing detail the grotesque acts he had committed against Billy. His words painted a macabre picture of brutality and cannibalism—acts that defy comprehension. This confession not only cemented Fish's legacy as an unrepentant monster but also underscored the depth of his depravity.

> *"I brought him to the Riker Ave. dumps. There is a house that stands alone, not far from where I took him ... I took the G boy there. Stripped him naked and tied his hands and feet and gagged him with a piece of dirty rag I picked out of the dump. Then I burned his clothes. Threw his shoes*

*in the dump. Then I walked back and took trolley to 59 St. at 2 A.M. and walked home from there. Next day about 2 P.M., I took tools, a good heavy cat-of-nine tails. Homemade. Short handle. Cut one of my belts in half, slit these half in six strips about 8 in. long. I whipped his bare behind till the blood ran from his legs. I cut off his ears – nose – slit his mouth from ear to ear. Gouged out his eyes. He was dead then. I stuck the knife in his belly and held my mouth to his body and drank his blood. I picked up four old potato sacks and gathered a pile of stones. Then I cut him up. I had a grip with me. I put his nose, ears and a few slices of his belly in the grip. Then I cut him thru the middle of his body. Just below his belly button. Then thru his legs about 2 in. below his behind. I put this in my grip with a lot of paper. I cut off the head – feet – arms – hands and the legs below the knee. This I put in sacks weighed with stones, tied the ends and threw them into the pools of slimy water you will see all along the road going to North Beach. Water is 3 to 4 ft. deep. They sank at once. I came home with my meat. I had the front of his body I liked best. His monkey and pee wees and a nice little fat behind to roast in the oven and eat. I made a stew out of his ears – nose – pieces of his face and belly. I put onions, carrots, turnips, celery, salt and pepper. It was good. Then I split the cheeks of his behind open, cut off his monkey and pee wees and washed them first. I put strips of bacon on each cheek of his behind and put in the oven. Then I picked 4 onions and when meat had roasted about 1/4 hr., I poured about a pint of water over it for gravy and put in the onions. At frequent intervals I basted his behind with a wooden spoon. So, the meat would be nice and juicy. In about 2 hr., it was nice and brown, cooked thru. I never ate any roast turkey that tasted half as good as his sweet fat little behind did. I ate every bit of the meat in about four days. His little monkey was as sweet as a nut, but his pee-wees I could not chew. Threw them in the toilet."*

Through these chilling accounts, we glimpse the terrifying nature of Albert Fish's crimes—events that continue to captivate and horrify the world today. His heinous acts serve as a stark reminder of the darkness that can lurk beneath the veneer of humanity.

**Trial and execution**

The trial of Albert Fish, a man whose crimes were as chilling as they were complex, commenced on March 11, 1935, in the quiet town of White Plains, New York. Presiding over the courtroom was Judge Frederick P. Close, while the prosecution was led by the determined

Westchester County Chief Assistant District Attorney, Elbert F. Gallagher. Opposing them was Fish's defense attorney, James Dempsey, a former prosecutor with the added political clout of being a one-time mayor of Peekskill, New York.

For ten grueling days, the courtroom became a theater of horror and disbelief as the details of Fish's heinous crimes were meticulously laid bare. Defending himself with a plea of insanity, Fish claimed to hear divine voices commanding him to murder children. Dempsey portrayed Fish as a "psychiatric phenomenon," citing a staggering array of sexually deviant behaviors, including sadism, masochism, and even cannibalism.

Central to the defense's argument was the testimony of Dr. Fredric Wertham, a psychiatrist renowned for his focus on child development. Over two exhaustive days, Wertham dissected Fish's distorted psyche, framing his obsession with biblical sacrifices as both a twisted penance and a misguided quest for atonement. Through Wertham's narrative, Fish emerged as a man who interpreted religious communion as an excuse for cannibalism, a disturbing reflection of his warped reality. When asked about Fish's mental state, Wertham concluded concisely and powerfully, "He is insane."

Yet, the prosecution countered with its own experts, challenging the notion of Fish's insanity. Menas Gregory, a former manager at Bellevue Hospital where Fish had been treated, argued that while Fish was undoubtedly abnormal, he was not insane by psychiatric standards. Further testimony from Charles Lambert and James Vavasour suggested that Fish's peculiar proclivities, shocking as they were, fell within the realm of common, albeit socially unacceptable, perversions.

The defense also presented Mary Nicholas, Fish's young stepdaughter, who recounted disturbing childhood games that hinted at Fish's deviant inclinations. However, despite the defense's efforts and the jurors' shared belief in Fish's insanity, the prevailing sentiment was one of justice—a justice demanding retribution. Thus, the jury returned a verdict of sanity and guilt, sealing Fish's fate with a sentence of death by electrocution.

On January 16, 1936, Fish met his end in the electric chair at Sing Sing Prison. Remarkably composed, he aided the executioner in positioning the electrodes upon his body. When questioned about his impending fate, Fish simply stated, "I don't even know why I'm here." The execution was fraught with rumors, including tales of needles embedded in his body causing a circuit malfunction—later debunked as mere legend.

In the aftermath, Fish's attorney, James Dempsey, confronted a media frenzy eager for a glimpse into the mind of one of history's most notorious criminals. Clutching Fish's final written statement, Dempsey refused to share its contents, describing it only as "the most filthy string of obscenities" he had ever encountered.

The tale of Albert Fish concluded, yet the echoes of his horrific deeds continue to haunt history. In his wake, Fish left a grim legacy, marked by the lives he shattered and the innocence he stole. His actions carved a dark path through the early 20th century.

## Fish's Victims

Albert Fish's shadow loomed heavily over the early 20th century, leaving a trail of victims—some known, others only speculated upon. In the tangled web of his macabre deeds, each victim and their grieving families warrant somber remembrance.

### Known Victims

From 1924 to 1928, Albert Fish's heinous acts claimed the lives of at least three innocent children:

- **Francis McDonnell**, an eight-year-old boy, vanished in the summer of 1924 on Long Island, New York. His disappearance marked the beginning of Fish's known atrocities.
- **Billy Gaffney**, just four years old, was last seen playing with a friend in New York City on February 11, 1927. His fate, sealed by Fish's monstrous hands, remains a haunting memory.
- **Grace Budd**, a ten-year-old girl, became one of Fish's most infamous cases. She was lured away on June 3, 1928, from her home in New York City, becoming a tragic emblem of his depravity.

### Suspected Victims

Despite Fish's denial of further murders, authorities suspected his involvement in numerous other unsolved cases. Detective William King harbored suspicions that Fish might be the elusive "Brooklyn Vampire," a predator who targeted the young and vulnerable around the New York City area.

- One such case involved **Yetta Abramowitz**, a twelve-year-old who was strangled and brutally beaten atop a Bronx apartment building on May 14, 1927. Witnesses reported seeing a man resembling Fish attempting to lure young girls into alleyways that same day.
- Then there was **Mary Ellen O'Connor**, a sixteen-year-old whose mutilated body was discovered near a property Fish had been painting in Far Rockaway, Queens, on February 15, 1932. Her murder remains a chilling mystery tied to Fish's sinister activities.

**Possible Victims**

Fish chillingly boasted of sexually assaulting over a hundred boys, many of whom were marginalized due to race or disability—a grim testament to his belief that justice would bypass these victims. In one of his most horrifying claims, he alleged he murdered a child in each of the twenty-three states where he resided.

Among these potential victims were:

- **Emma Richardson**, a five-year-old whose life was cut short on October 3, 1926.
- **Emil Aalling**, a four-year-old taken on July 13, 1930.
- **Robin Jane Liu**, a six-year-old lost on May 2, 1931.
- **Benjamin Collings**, who at seventeen, faced an untimely death on December 15, 1932.

Few figures evoke as much horror and revulsion as Albert Fish. Often regarded as one of the most depraved serial killers of all time, Fish's heinous acts defy comprehension and challenge the very limits of human morality. While his severe mental illness is undeniable, many argue that justice was served with his execution, as his crimes left a scar on the collective conscience that can never fully heal.

Fish's story is a haunting illustration of the malevolence that can lie dormant within the human psyche, waiting to surface in the most terrifying ways. His confessions, both chilling and revolting, offer a glimpse into a mind twisted beyond repair, driven by urges that defy rational understanding. The suspected breadth of his crimes suggests an insatiable appetite for suffering, making him a specter whose legacy is one of unrelenting darkness.

This narrative serves as a sobering reminder of the evil that can exist behind the guise of normalcy, prompting us to ponder the complexities of human nature and the depths of depravity to which it can sink. Fish's tale forces us to confront not only the lives irrevocably altered by his actions but also our own understanding of justice and redemption. It is a chilling chronicle that compels us to reflect on the fragile boundary between sanity and madness, normality and monstrosity.

# CHAPTER THREE

## WHAT HAPPENED TO D.B. COOPER?

Not all enthralling true crime tales involve gruesome acts or sinister plots. Some captivate the imagination by weaving threads of mystery and intrigue, with characters who vanish into the dark of night without a trace. Such is the case with D.B. Cooper, an enduring mystery that has puzzled armchair sleuths for decades.

### The Fateful Day

On November 24, 1971, an unremarkable man who introduced himself as Dan Cooper approached the Northwest Orient Airlines counter at Portland International Airport. He purchased a one-way ticket to Seattle, Washington, paying in cash—a decision that would forever embroil him in one of the most perplexing unsolved cases in the FBI's archives.

## An Ordinary Man, An Extraordinary Plan

Dan Cooper, mistakenly dubbed "D.B. Cooper" due to a media blunder, seemed the epitome of an average businessman in his mid-40s. Clad in a suit, accented with a black tie and a crisp white shirt, he boarded Northwest Orient Airlines Flight 305, a Boeing 727, without attracting undue attention. Once seated, he ordered a bourbon and soda, blending in seamlessly with his fellow travelers. Yet beneath this veneer of normalcy lay the blueprint for a daring and audacious act that would soon capture the world's attention.

## The Calm Before the Storm

Cooper's demeanor was calm and composed as he settled into his seat. His unassuming behavior persisted as the aircraft taxied and took off, marking the beginning of a flight that would become infamous for its unexpected turn. What followed was a meticulously planned heist, executed with precision and leaving law enforcement agencies grappling with unanswered questions and an elusive perpetrator who vanished as mysteriously as he appeared.

Thus began the legend of D.B. Cooper—a story not defined by bloodshed, but by a sheer audacity and an enigmatic escape that continues to challenge investigators and intrigue the public to this very day. The mystery endures, inviting us to peer into the shadows of history and ponder the identity and fate of the man who dared to defy gravity —and the law.

## The Hijacking Unfolds

It was a routine afternoon on November 24, 1971, aboard Northwest Orient Airlines Flight 305. Business travelers and holidaymakers settled in for what they expected to be an ordinary flight. Among them was Dan Cooper - calm and composed, the picture of a typical businessman awaiting takeoff. But as the plane cruised through the skies, his demeanor took on a more sinister edge.

Shortly after 3 p.m., Cooper caught the attention of a flight attendant, urging her to come closer. He discreetly slipped her a note, which she initially tucked away without reading, assuming it was just another flirtatious gesture. But Cooper's voice, steady and cold, insisted she read it immediately. She unfolded the paper to find a chilling message —he had a bomb in his briefcase.

Without raising alarm, the attendant sat beside him, as he had asked. Cooper quietly opened his attaché case, revealing a jumbled array of wires and red sticks, hinting at the deadly potential it contained. The stark contrast between his understated manner and the gravity of his threat left no room for doubt. He dictated his demands for the captain—a staggering $200,000 in cash, equivalent to nearly $1.5 million today, and four parachutes. His instructions were clear, and she hurried to the cockpit, the weight of his words spurring her every step.

## The Exchange

Against the backdrop of dusk, Seattle-Tacoma International Airport was bathed in a soft glow. It was here that Dan Cooper's meticulously crafted plan began to unfold. With an unnerving calm, he orchestrated the release of 36 passengers, each now free from the ordeal that had begun hours earlier. Yet, for the crew remaining on board, their harrowing experience was only just beginning.

With the ransom money secured and parachutes carefully stowed, Cooper tightened his grip on the airliner, transforming it into an airborne fortress. His next demand? A flight bound for Mexico City, with a necessary refueling stop in Reno, Nevada. The remaining crew, caught up in this unfolding drama, had no choice but to comply with their captor's commands.

In what would soon become an indelible chapter in aviation history, Cooper's audacious plot was on the brink of climax.

**Into the Night**

With its engines roaring to life, the aircraft once again ascended into the night sky. Somewhere over the shadowy expanses of southwestern Washington, Cooper made his daring move. Just over thirty minutes into the flight, he lowered the rear stairs of the plane and, with the ransom money strapped to his body, leaped into the inky abyss—a night cloaked in rain and darkness. The pilots, following protocol, landed the aircraft safely, but Cooper had vanished without a trace.

His disappearance between Mt. Rainier and northern Portland created an instant legend. The hijacker had ordered the pilot to open the aircraft's rear door before making his escape.

Yet, as Special Agent Larry Carr noted in a 2007 case update, "No experienced parachutist would have jumped in the pitch-black night, in the rain, with a 200-mile-an-hour wind in his face, wearing loafers and a trench coat. It was simply too risky." Cooper's choice to jump with a reserve chute—one that was sewn shut and only meant for training—only added to the mystery, suggesting a deadly oversight or sheer desperation.

Thus, an audacious tale of high-stakes intrigue and an untraceable escape was born.

**The Aftermath**

In the immediate chaos that followed the infamous skyjacking, the FBI sprang into action with a sweeping investigation known as Operation NORJAK—short for Northwest Hijacking. This high-stakes operation was launched even before the jetliner touched down, as agents scrambled to piece together one of aviation history's most perplexing mysteries. The bureau left no stone unturned. They carefully combed over every inch of the aircraft, hoping to uncover any detail that might lead them closer to the notorious hijacker known as D.B. Cooper.

NORJAK was not just an operation; it was a relentless pursuit of truth. Over the years, agents conducted exhaustive interviews with hundreds of individuals and chased down leads from coast to coast. The team's dedication was unwavering as they meticulously analyzed every shred of evidence. Their determination led to narrowing a daunting list of over 800 suspects down to just 24 individuals.

Yet, despite the intensity of their efforts and the promising leads that emerged, the man behind the alias of D.B. Cooper remained as shadowy and anonymous as the night he vanished. His true identity and what ultimately became of him continued to elude some of the nation's sharpest minds.

**Theories and Suspects**

Among the myriad of suspects, Richard Floyd McCoy often stands out due to his arrest for a remarkably similar crime. Less than five months after Cooper's audacious hijacking and parachute escape, McCoy executed a comparable heist, parachuting from a plane with ransom in hand. For a time, investigators considered him a prime suspect. However, despite the striking similarities, discrepancies in physical descriptions and other critical details eventually led authorities to rule him out as the elusive Cooper.

The question of whether Cooper survived his daring leap into the unknown has spawned endless speculation and theories. Evidence suggests he may not have been a seasoned skydiver, as the parachute he used was non-steerable, making navigation nearly impossible. Furthermore, his attire—a business suit and regular shoes—was ill-suited for a perilous jump into the wilderness on a cold, wet November evening.

November 24, 1971, was a typical night for the Pacific Northwest, characterized by chilling weather and relentless rain. Cooper's jump occurred sometime after 8 p.m., plunging him into darkness shrouded by dense cloud cover at 5,000 feet. His likely landing spot lay in the rugged terrain of southwestern Washington, a region battered by an ongoing storm of rain and snow.

While the exact elevation of Cooper's landing site remains unknown, weather data offers chilling insights. At Stampede Pass, situated about 100-150 miles north, steady snowfall blanketed the landscape, accumulating 27 inches by November 29. The temperatures lingered in the frigid upper 20s to 30 degrees Fahrenheit, painting a grim picture of Cooper's chances for survival.

The FBI's focus centered on the area around Lake Merwin, where terrain elevations varied from 2,000 to 2,500 feet. Yet, if the wind carried him eastward, Cooper faced even higher elevations. Reports from Portland confirm that the heavy precipitation extended into southern Washington and northern Oregon, ensuring that Cooper would have encountered either a snowstorm or torrential rain, depending on his final resting place.

In the inhospitable wilderness, Cooper was left with little more than his suit and shoes—hardly the equipment needed for survival in such harsh conditions. With no provisions for warmth, fire, or shelter, he would have been soaked from the jump, exposed to relentless rain or snow, and struggling against the unforgiving elements. If he managed to survive and vanish without a trace, it would not only be one of the greatest heists in history but also an extraordinary survival story.

However, if the odds were against him, his tale serves as a cautionary reminder of nature's unpredictability, emphasizing the importance of preparation and awareness before venturing into the unknown.

A significant clue emerged in 1980 when a young boy named Brian Ingram made a startling discovery. While digging a fire pit in the sandy banks of the Columbia River at Tena Bar, north of Portland, Ingram unearthed three bundles of decaying twenty-dollar bills. The total amount —$5,800—matched the serial numbers of the ransom money, marking the first evidence linked to Cooper since his disappearance.

The discovery ignited fresh curiosity and debate among "Cooper Hunters," who speculated on how the money arrived at the riverbank. Theories abounded, adding fuel to the legend of D.B. Cooper and his fate.

**What Was D.B. Cooper's Fate?**

The mystery of D.B. Cooper has sparked debates worldwide. Forums and online communities buzz with theories about the destiny of the elusive hijacker, driven by a few intriguing questions that remain unanswered to this day. Several theories have been dissected by the group, "Citizen Sleuths", a dedicated team of online researchers with backgrounds in crime investigations.

**The Jump into Uncertainty**

One of the most hotly debated topics is whether Cooper could have survived his dramatic leap from the plane. Experts are divided; some seasoned skydivers suggest that an amateur would not have survived such a daring jump, whereas others claim that with just a handful of practice jumps, survival was plausible. The harsh weather conditions that night only add to the uncertainty. Despite thorough searches, no body or parachute has been discovered, leaving Cooper's fate shrouded in mystery.

**The Skydiver's Skillset**

Determining Cooper's level of expertise in skydiving presents its own set of puzzles. His request for "front and back parachutes" hints at inexperience, yet his refusal of parachute instructions suggests confidence and familiarity. The choice of a non-steerable military parachute raises more questions than answers—was it a novice error or a calculated decision due to its ability to endure high-speed jumps? While he donned the parachute with apparent proficiency, his selection of a non-functional reserve chute seems to contradict this. This blend of seemingly opposing actions keeps investigators guessing about his true capabilities.

**The Tena Bar Discovery**

In 1980, a young boy stumbled upon a bundle of decaying bills along the Columbia River's Tena Bar—an unexpected clue in an otherwise cold case. This discovery is puzzling, given that it's located 20 miles from the theorized drop zone near Ariel, Washington. Several theories attempt to explain this mystery. The Washougal Washdown Theory posits that the money traveled through smaller rivers into the Columbia. Alternatively, some speculate that the FBI's flight path was incorrect, allowing Cooper to land directly at Tena Bar and hide the money himself. There's also the possibility that Cooper, or an accomplice, intentionally buried the money to mislead authorities. Geologist Dr. Leonard Palmer's analysis suggested the cash settled into newly deposited dredge sand, indicating it may have traveled from upstream, though the intact rubber bands challenge this timeline.

**Mysteries of the Money**

How three bundles of cash remained together for years, only to be uncovered buried, remains a point of intrigue. Theories range from the bundles being protected by a bank bag, which later disintegrated, to Cooper losing the money upon his landing. Some even suggest a third party could have buried it there for reasons unknown.

**The Condition of the Cash**

The condition of the recovered money, with edges worn and holes present, prompts questions about its time spent in the elements. Could roots, river currents, or dredging have contributed to its deterioration?

**The Flight Path Conundrum**

The official flight path, as mapped in the FBI archives, lacks critical details such as its creator and date. Speculation suggests it was derived from radar data and flight recorder analyses. However, this path does not align with Tena Bar or the Washougal area. The discovery at Tena Bar forces a reconsideration of the flight path, suggesting Cooper may have jumped or the plane flew over a different trajectory than initially believed.

### The Local Connection

Cooper's recognition of Tacoma from the air suggests familiarity with the region, yet it raises suspicions about his origins. Some speculate he was a local; however, the unique request for "negotiable American currency" implies he might have been an outsider unfamiliar with American vernacular.

### The Suspect Dilemma

Despite countless investigations and potential leads, none of the current suspects fit the D.B. Cooper profile convincingly. Experts surmise Cooper might have been employed in fields related to metalworking or chemical processing, but doubt lingers over whether any of the FBI's suspects are the real hijacker.

### A Mystery That Endures

The case of D.B. Cooper is one of those rare enigmas that has captivated both seasoned law enforcement and amateur sleuths for decades.

Despite exhaustive investigations by the FBI and countless theories spun by amateur investigators around the globe, the case remains unsolved. D.B. Cooper's daring leap from the aircraft into the dense forests of southwestern Washington has left an indelible mark on the true crime world. Each attempt to uncover the truth only adds layers of complexity to the narrative, leaving behind a trail of unanswered questions.

Did Cooper survive that perilous jump into the rugged wilderness? Is he living somewhere under a new identity, having successfully eluded capture with his ill-gotten gains? Or did he meet a different fate, swallowed by the vast and unforgiving terrain below?

The allure of the D.B. Cooper story lies not only in its mystery but also in its tantalizing what-ifs. In a case devoid of violence or injury, many find themselves secretly rooting for the enigmatic hijacker. The notion that Cooper might have managed to start anew, free from the constraints of his former life, taps into a universal yearning for reinvention. With a world often feeling overwhelming, who hasn't dreamed of parachuting into a fresh beginning, unburdened by the past?

This idea, the possibility of a successful escape and reinvention, is perhaps why the legend of D.B. Cooper refuses to fade. It challenges our notions of justice and law, urging us to contemplate the thin line between crime and adventure. While the truth about D.B. Cooper remains elusive, the mystery continues to beckon us, whispering its unanswered questions and daring us to solve its riddle.

# CHAPTER FOUR

## THE MYSTERIOUS MURDER OF ROSE HARSENT

Unraveling the threads of history often reveals tales both captivating and chilling, yet few can rival the murder of Rose Harsent. For more than a century, this case has bewitched historians, its unsolved nature adding an unsettling allure to its already grim narrative.

On the turbulent night of May 31, 1902, the serene village of Peasenhall in Suffolk, England, was thrust into infamy. The tranquil setting was suddenly disrupted by a violent storm, providing the perfect ominous backdrop for what would become one of the most intriguing murder mysteries of the era.

The murder took place in an unassuming village house, nestled directly across from the familiar hubbub of Emmett's Store. The crime itself bore the hallmarks of a classic 'country house' murder, steeped in mystery and executed close to the witching hour amid the furious storm —a storyline that could have been plucked from the pages of a gothic novel. Such a setting, combined with the unexplainable events that unfurled, wove together a tapestry of suspense that continues to captivate.

---

The early 1900s painted Peasenhall as a quintessential English village, where the rhythm of daily life followed the gentle cadence of its cobbled lanes and the industrious hum of its residents. The men of Peasenhall largely found their livelihoods at Smyth's Seed Drill Works while spiritually anchoring themselves at the Primitive Methodist Chapel in the nearby village of Sibton. It was within this chapel's walls that 22-year-old Rose Anne Harsent found solace. A dutiful domestic servant to Mr. and Mrs. Crisp at Providence House, Rose was known not only for her work but for her involvement in the village's spiritual life.

Beyond her household responsibilities, Rose was a familiar figure at the Wesleyan Methodist Chapel, colloquially dubbed the Doctor's Chapel. It was here that Rose—while meticulously tending to her cleaning duties—allegedly encountered the charismatic William Gardiner, the esteemed – and married - choirmaster of the Primitive Methodist Chapel. His presence, particularly during Rose's solitary hours of work, did not go unnoticed. Eyewitnesses, including Alphonso Skinner and a "Mr. Wright", claimed to have seen Gardiner enter the chapel during Rose's cleaning sessions. This sparked a wildfire of rumors that swept through Peasenhall, casting long shadows of suspicion that reached even the ears of Gardiner's wife.

Despite the ensuing church inquiry spearheaded by the Rev. John Guy, tangible evidence remained elusive. The whispers of scandal refused to be silenced, however. The allegations were incendiary enough that Gardiner felt compelled to threaten legal retribution against any who dared to tarnish his reputation further.

In this deeply rooted rural community, where personal reputations were as cherished as they were fragile, the entangled lives of Rose Harsent and William Gardiner became fodder for speculation and gossip—a spectral presence that loomed ominously over the quiet village, long after the stormy night had passed. The question that still haunts Peasenhall is whether the mysterious murder was a consequence of these whispered intrigues or if a darker force lay behind the veil of thunder and shadow.

**Murder and Investigation**

On the morning of June 1st, 1902, the residents of Peasenhall, Suffolk, England, awoke to what should have been a typical serene Sunday. Yet, this day would mark the beginning of a haunting chapter in their village's history—a day marred by tragedy and mystery that would send ripples of fear and curiosity through the community.

The scene was Providence House, where William Harsent, a respected member of society, walked into his own personal nightmare. In the dim light of the kitchen, he found his daughter, Rose Harsent, sprawled lifelessly on the cold floor. The horrific sight before him was enough to chill the blood of even the most seasoned investigator. Rose lay in a pool of her own blood, her throat cruelly slit —a gruesome testament to the violence that had befallen her.

Every detail of the crime spoke of an unbridled fury. Her shoulders bore deep, savage gashes, as though the assailant had been driven by an uncontrollable rage. Stab wounds peppered her body, each one a silent cry for justice. Yet the horror did not end here. Her nightdress, once a simple garment, was now a darkened, charred remnant—a grim indication that someone had tried to obliterate the evidence by fire.

In the immediate aftermath, whispers of suicide began to circulate among the villagers, a notion quickly dismissed as the evidence unfolded. The brutal nature of her injuries told a story far removed from self-infliction. No, this was not a tragic act of desperation; it was murder, cold and calculated.

The investigation took an unexpected turn when it emerged that Rose was six months pregnant. This revelation added a layer of complexity and pathos to the crime, intertwining the fate of her unborn child with her own tragic demise. This new piece of information cast a long shadow over the case, deepening the sense of loss and outrage.

Soon, attention turned to William Gardiner, a man enmeshed in a web of rumors and speculation. Village gossip hinted at a forbidden relationship between Gardiner and Rose, with whispers suggesting he could be the father of her unborn child. Just days after Rose's death, on June 3rd, 1902, Gardiner found himself ensnared by suspicion, though concrete evidence was scant. The weight of circumstantial clues and relentless village talk pressed heavily upon him, painting him as a man with much to hide.

This investigation unfolded much like a tragic narrative, each revelation casting a stark light on Peasenhall's darkest day. It was a tale steeped in passion, betrayal, and the desperate lengths one might go to in order to conceal the truth. With every step, the mystery deepened.

### The Case Against Gardiner

In the dim light of a crime scene, the evidence lay scattered, whispering secrets to those willing to listen. The murder of Rose had left a ripple of shock and intrigue across town, and Gardiner found himself at the heart of the storm. Though the police lacked an unequivocal piece of evidence—a smoking gun—several clues pointed ominously in Gardiner's direction.

### A Prescription for Suspicion

Among the scattered clues at the scene was an innocuous-looking prescription bottle. Yet this was no ordinary bottle; it bore the names of Gardiner and his wife, its contents replaced with paraffin. Nearby, crumpled and stained letters spoke of secret meetings and whispered promises. One letter in particular stood out, a pulse of desperation embedded in its words:

> *"Dear R, I will try to see you tonight at 12 o'clock at your place. If you put a light in your window at ten for about ten minutes, then you can put it out again."*

The police could only surmise that this letter was penned by someone with motives darker than the night it described. Their suspicions grew stronger when they discovered a newspaper at the scene—one that neither Rose nor her employers subscribed to, but that Gardiner did.

### The Gruesome Discovery

The post-mortem examination painted a grim picture of Rose's final moments. Her body bore the marks of a violent struggle—bruises, stab wounds, and a final, cruel cut to her throat. Her hands, marked with defensive wounds, spoke of a fierce fight against her assailant. The heart-wrenching discovery that Rose had been six months pregnant at the time of her death added another layer of tragedy to the case.

### Piecing Together Motive

The authorities speculated on Gardiner's potential motive. Could he have fathered Rose's unborn child, jeopardizing his respectable facade? Was the prescription bottle a careless mistake, or a deliberate taunt? And what of the handwriting on the incriminating letter that bore an uncanny resemblance to Gardiner's own?

### The Witnesses Speak

Witnesses added fuel to the growing fire. One neighbor recounted seeing Gardiner standing outside his home one evening, his gaze fixed intently on Providence House, where a light flickered in an upstairs window—a detail eerily reminiscent of the letter's instructions. Another spoke of a bonfire in Gardiner's yard on the very day Rose's body was discovered. Was he simply clearing yard debris, or erasing evidence of his guilt?

### The Bloody Knife

Yet perhaps the most damning piece of evidence was a small hinged knife, carried habitually by Gardiner. Upon closer inspection, the knife hinge revealed traces of blood, a chilling testament to its possible use. Gardiner, of course, maintained his innocence, flatly denying any involvement in Rose's murder. But as the pieces came together, the police felt compelled to act, charging Gardiner with the heinous crime.

Thus, in a web of circumstantial evidence and shadowed truth, the case against Gardiner was set to unfold, each detail deepening a mystery for authorities to unravel.

### Trial and Aftermath

In Peasenhall, where cobblestones whispered secrets underfoot, the Gardiner family resided in quiet prominence. Their home lay on the bustling main street, forever overshadowed by the imposing silhouette of Providence House. Gardiner, a man respected yet enigmatic, was entwined with a dark narrative that would forever alter his life.

Gardiner's trial morphed into a public spectacle, drawing throngs of eager spectators to the hallowed halls of Ipswich Assizes at the County Hall. The anticipation was palpable as the gavel fell on November 7, 1902, marking the commencement of the first trial. Presiding over the event was Sir William Grantham, whose presence set the tone for three arduous days of deliberation. Yet, the story refused to conclude. A second trial was summoned on January 20, 1903, under the watchful eye of Sir John Compton Lawrance, each session a meticulous unravelling of the tangled web of events.

Ernest Wild, with his piercing rhetoric and unyielding dedication, stood staunchly in Gardiner's defense. His words painted a picture of doubt and persuasion. Opposing him was the indomitable Henry Fielding Dickens, whose commanding presence and sharp intellect led a prosecution steeped in determination.

Both trials culminated in deadlocks—the first jury divided eleven to one in favor of guilt, the second mirrored the uncertainty but swung towards innocence. In an era when a single dissenting voice could sway the course of justice, the prosecution, faced with such impasse, issued a writ of nolle prosequi. It left Gardiner in a paradoxical state, a man judged yet never absolved—a specter of culpability lingering without closure.

Gardiner's life trudged onward, shadowed by whispers of guilt and the relentless passage of time. He passed away in 1941, his name eternally tethered to Rose Harsent's murder. The case, though long dormant, was resurrected in modern memory through BBC One's "Julian Fellowes Investigates: A Most Mysterious Murder." Fellowes, with his knack for the dramatic, postulated that perhaps the truth lay with Gardiner's wife, perhaps driven by jealousy and constrained by a rigid society. Her whispered confession, lost to the winds of time, might have surfaced had her husband been condemned.

The Peasenhall mystery captivates the world with its enduring elusiveness. This tale, a haunting blend of mystery and historical allure, draws us into the quaint yet shadowy corners of early 20th-century rural England. Here, communities were tightly knit, their lives intertwined by bonds of trust and shared belief systems that seemed unbreakable—until the fateful night in 1902 shattered this idyllic facade.

In pondering Rose Harsent's story, we are left to marvel at the allure of mysteries that refuse resolution, navigating the delicate balance between fact and the unknown. This is the essence of true crime, where the search for truth intertwines with the insatiable curiosity of the human spirit, leaving an indelible mark on all who dare to venture into its depths.

# CHAPTER FIVE

## THE LINDBERGH BABY KIDNAPPING

The Lindbergh Baby Kidnapping is one of America's most notorious crimes, where Charles and Anne Lindbergh's infant son, Charles Jr., was abducted from their home in 1932. This tragic event sparked a nationwide frenzy and led to a complex investigation, the arrest of Bruno Hauptmann, and ongoing debates about justice and societal impact. It remains a poignant chapter in American history, highlighting the intersection of fame, tragedy, and media sensationalism.

---

### The Evening of March 1, 1932

The night started like any other at the Lindbergh residence. Despite the chilly weather, the family was in high spirits. Charles Lindbergh, the "Lone Eagle," had recently returned from yet another successful speaking tour, and Anne Morrow Lindbergh had been working on her latest book project. Their son, Charles Jr., affectionately known as "Little Lindy," had just turned 20 months old and was the apple of his parents' eyes.

At around 7:30 PM, the family settled into their usual evening routine. Little Lindy was tucked into his crib by the family nurse, Betty Gow, in the nursery on the second floor. The Lindberghs then retired to their respective activities—Charles to his study to catch up on correspondence, and Anne to soak in the bath before bed.

By 9 PM, the household was silent, save for the occasional creak of the old wooden floors. Nothing seemed out of the ordinary. Yet, unbeknownst to the Lindberghs, a sinister plot was unfolding just outside their home.

**The Kidnapping**

Just after the clock struck 10 PM, Betty Gow made her final check on the baby for the night. What she found terrified her to her core. Little Lindy's crib was empty, and the window was ajar, allowing a chilling gust of night air to fill the room. Panic set in as she realized the unthinkable—Little Lindy was gone. She raised the alarm, her voice trembling with fear.

Charles Lindbergh dashed to the nursery, his heart racing, a blend of fear and disbelief clouding his mind. Frantically, he began searching the room for any sign of his son. Then, his eyes landed on a note left precariously on the windowsill. It was a ransom note, hastily scribbled, demanding a hefty $50,000 for the safe return of their beloved child.

The ransom note itself was a cryptic piece of art, scrawled in haphazard handwriting with glaring grammatical errors and peculiar spellings.

The note read:

> *"Dear Sir!*
> *Have 50.000$ redy 25 000$ in 20$ bills 15000$ in 10$ bills and 10000$ in 5$ bills After 2–4 days we will inform you were to deliver the mony. We warn you for making anyding public or for notify the Police the child is in gut care. Indication for all letters are Singnature and 3 hohls."*

Beneath the oddly-phrased demands lay a strange symbol—two blue circles intersecting a red circle, pierced by a hole in the red center and flanked by two additional holes.

With dread tightening in his chest, Charles immediately contacted the police and their family lawyer. The authorities arrived within hours, setting off a whirlwind of activity that would soon captivate the nation. The Lindbergh Baby Kidnapping was not simply a personal tragedy—it had already escalated into a national crisis.

**The Investigation**

The search began with a rigor that only the direst circumstances could summon. Police from Hopewell Borough, in concert with the New Jersey State Police, swept through the Lindbergh home and its surrounding grounds, their flashlights piercing the midnight darkness in desperate pursuit of any clue that might shed light on the abduction.

As the clock struck midnight, a fingerprint expert would meticulously examine the ransom note and the ladder used in the crime. Yet, the findings were disheartening. No viable fingerprints or footprints surfaced. It seemed the kidnapper, or kidnappers, had donned gloves and covered their shoes with cloth, ensuring no trace was left behind. The baby's room bore no adult fingerprints, yet the delicate prints of the infant lingered there—a haunting reminder of the life so suddenly disrupted.

Forensic experts scrutinized the ransom letter and concluded it was penned by a single individual, likely foreign, whose grasp of English was minimal. The Federal Bureau of Investigation enlisted a sketch artist to capture the essence of the suspected kidnapper, hoping a portrait would lead to a breakthrough.

Meanwhile, the ladder used in the nefarious act underwent an exhaustive examination. Though poorly constructed, it bore the telltale signs of someone familiar with woodworking. With no fingerprints left behind to guide them, investigators turned their attention to the wood itself. They analyzed slivers to determine the types of wood, the pattern of nail holes, and whether it was crafted indoors or outdoors. This minutiae would later prove pivotal in the trial against the man accused of orchestrating the kidnapping.

On March 2, 1932, FBI Director J. Edgar Hoover reached out to the Trenton, New Jersey Police Department, offering the agency's full arsenal of resources. Though the FBI lacked federal jurisdiction at the time, President Herbert

Hoover soon remedied this. By May 13, 1932, he declared the FBI at the disposal of New Jersey authorities, entrusting them with the investigation's orchestration and execution.

In an effort to galvanize public cooperation, the New Jersey State Police announced a $25,000 reward—equivalent to over half a million dollars today—for any information leading to a resolution.

Enter Gaston B. Means, a man of dubious repute. On March 4, 1932, he approached Evalyn Walsh McLean, claiming he could facilitate the return of the Lindbergh baby. Mrs. McLean was an American mining heiress and socialite, famous for being the owner of the 45-carat Hope Diamond. McLean was a close friend of the Lindberghs, and was eager to do anything she could to help bring their child back to them.

Gaston B. Means spun a tale of prior knowledge in the case, asserting he had been propositioned to join a "major kidnapping" weeks before the crime and that a friend of his was the culprit. Convincing Mrs. McLean of his sincerity, Means secured $100,000 from her, arguing the ransom had doubled. Day after day, McLean awaited the child's return, but her hope turned to disillusionment. When Means refused to return the money, she reported him to authorities. He was sentenced to fifteen years for embezzlement.

In a tragic turn, Violet Sharpe, a household servant under suspicion, took her own life on June 10 before a fourth round of questioning. Her involvement was later dismissed, as alibi evidence confirmed her whereabouts on the night of the abduction.

By October 1933, President Franklin D. Roosevelt proclaimed that the FBI would assume control of the investigation, cementing their role in one of America's most infamous cases.

## The Ransom and Discovery

On April 2$^{nd}$, 1932, precisely a month after the heart-wrenching kidnapping, a glimmer of hope emerged. An intermediary, the enigmatic Dr. John F. Condon, successfully arranged the ransom payment. Charles Lindbergh himself handed over the money, clutching onto the fragile promise delivered in a note. It claimed that Little Lindy was hidden away on a boat named "Nellie" anchored somewhere off the coast of Massachusetts.

But hope began to wane as days stretched into weeks, and weeks languished into months without a whisper from the kidnappers. The absence of further communication gnawed at the Lindberghs' souls. Then, the most dreadful news broke on May 12, 1932. The lifeless body of Charles Augustus Lindbergh Jr. was stumbled upon by a truck driver in a secluded forest, just a stone's throw from the Lindbergh residence. The grim discovery revealed that the child had been dead for over two agonizing months, the cause of death—a brutal blow to the head.

The nation was enveloped in sorrow. This tragedy had not just shattered the Lindbergh family; it had plunged America's collective conscience into mourning. The quest for justice became relentless, and the investigation's tempo surged with renewed urgency.

## The Arrest of Bruno Richard Hauptmann

Two years later - in September 1934 – a breakthrough came. A marked bill from the ransom payment surfaced at a gas station in New York City. The attendant, sharpened by curiosity, noted that the man who passed the bill was behind the wheel of a vehicle with New Jersey plates. This seemingly innocuous detail led law enforcement to the doorstep of Bruno Richard Hauptmann, a German immigrant with a shadowy past.

Hauptmann's arrest triggered a cascade of revelations. A thorough search of his home unearthed a substantial stash of the ransom money concealed in his garage. Handwriting experts scrutinized the ransom notes, their keen eyes affirming that the penmanship bore a striking resemblance to Hauptmann's own scrawl. The evidence mounted, weighty and condemning. Hauptmann was soon charged with the heinous kidnapping and murder of Charles Lindbergh Jr.

## The Trial of the Century

The trial of Bruno Richard Hauptmann, which commenced in January 1935, wasn't merely a legal proceeding; it was an event that captivated the entire nation. This "Trial of the Century" turned the sleepy town of Flemington, New Jersey, into the buzzing epicenter of global media attention. Reporters flocked from every corner of the world, their cameras and notepads ready to capture every twist and turn of this sensational case. The courtroom itself became a theater, packed with a motley audience of eager spectators, all anticipating the high drama that was about to unfold.

The prosecution built its case meticulously, brick by brick, turning the spotlight on the damning pieces of evidence that seemed to seal Hauptmann's fate. The ransom money discovered in his possession served as a glaring red flag, while expert handwriting analysis further tightened the noose around his neck. Among the witnesses, none stood out more than Dr. Condon, whose testimony was both riveting and chilling. He pointed to Hauptmann as the enigmatic figure he had encountered during the shadowy ransom negotiations.

Throughout this ordeal, Hauptmann clung stubbornly to his claim of innocence. He insisted the tainted money had been left to him by a deceased associate named Isidor Fisch, a figure shrouded in mystery and conveniently unable to testify. Yet, in the eyes of the jury, these assertions rang hollow. The narrative spun by the defense lacked the substance and credibility needed to shift the scales of justice.

Ultimately, on a cold day in February—February 13, 1935, to be precise—the jury delivered its verdict. Bruno Richard Hauptmann was found guilty of first-degree murder, a verdict that carried the ultimate penalty. With that sentence, the curtain fell on one of the most dramatic trials in American history, but the echoes of its proceedings continued to reverberate.

## Appeals

Upon his conviction, Hauptmann was swiftly sentenced to death. His attorneys immediately appealed to the New Jersey Court of Errors and Appeals, the state's highest court at the time. New Jersey Governor Harold G. Hoffman, skeptical of the trial's outcome, secretly visited Hauptmann and urged a continued investigation, suspecting the crime was not a solo act. Despite the Governor's efforts, Hauptmann's appeals were denied.

In late January 1936, Governor Hoffman highlighted the need for a thorough investigation, convinced that the crime was too complex for a single perpetrator. However, as media speculation about another reprieve grew, Hauptmann's final appeal for clemency was refused on March 30, 1936. The legal avenues closed, and the final grand jury investigation ended without new charges.

## The Execution and The Aftermath

Facing his fate with stoic defiance, Hauptmann rejected an offer for a confession from a Hearst newspaper and turned down a last-minute deal to commute his sentence. On April 3, 1936, he was executed in the electric chair.

Even after his death, controversy surrounded his case. Suspicions of misconduct during the investigation, including witness tampering and planted evidence, lingered. In the 1980s, Anna Hauptmann tirelessly pursued justice, suing the state of New Jersey twice for her husband's wrongful execution. Despite her efforts, her claims were dismissed, and she continued her fight until her death in 1994, still determined to clear his name.

Hauptmann's trial and execution remain a haunting reminder of a case that captured the world's attention, leaving behind lingering doubts and unresolved questions.

**Enduring Mysteries and Legacy**

While the legal proceedings of this case focused heavily on Bruno Richard Hauptmann and the prosecution's efforts to secure his conviction, the underlying sorrow of a family torn apart by grief remains palpable. The spotlight on Hauptmann's potential innocence complicates the narrative, suggesting that perhaps, in the pursuit of justice, the true depths of this heartbreak were overshadowed. The life of a beloved child, snuffed out in an act of unimaginable cruelty, serves as the central horror of this story, compelling us to reflect on the innocence lost and the profound impact of such a crime on a society grappling with its own fragility. This case, steeped in mystery and controversy, continually challenges us to acknowledge both the suffering of the Lindbergh family and the complex moral questions it raises about justice and accountability.

# CHAPTER SIX

## THE MYSTERY OF LITTLE LORD FAUNTLEROY

In the quiet town of Waukesha, Wisconsin, a grim discovery made headlines in 1921 and has stumped investigators for over a century. The remains of a young boy, impeccably dressed in expensive clothing, were found lifeless in a quarry pond. This unknown child would come to be known as Little Lord Fauntleroy, a name borrowed from a well-dressed character in a popular children's book of the era. Unlike the innocent narrative of the book, this story was one steeped in sorrow and mystery.

---

The morning of March 8, 1921, began like any other for the residents of Waukesha. But the day took a dark turn when a local quarry worker stumbled upon the lifeless body of a young boy floating in the chilly waters of the town's abandoned quarry pond. Clad in a fine blouse, dark brown corduroy knickerbockers, black stockings, and a gray sweater, the boy appeared to be around five to seven years old. His attire, both stylish and expensive, suggested that he came from a family of means. Yet, his identity and the circumstances leading up to his tragic end were shrouded in mystery.

The authorities, unable to identify the boy, began referring to him as Little Lord Fauntleroy. This moniker was inspired by the character from Frances Hodgson Burnett's 1886 children's novel, "Little Lord Fauntleroy," which told the tale of a young, well-to-do boy with a heart of gold. However, unlike the fictional Lord Fauntleroy who enjoyed a life of privilege and happiness, this real-life child's story was marred by tragedy and unanswered questions.

**Discovery**

The morning of March 8, 1921, began like any other for John Brlich, an employee of the O'Laughlin Stone Company in Waukesha, Wisconsin. However, his routine stroll near the quarry pond was interrupted by a sight that would haunt the town for years to come. Floating amidst the serene waters was the lifeless body of a small boy.

Horrified, Brlich immediately alerted Waukesha County Sheriff Clarence Keebler, who then contacted County Coroner L.F. Lee. Together, the two officials hurried to the scene, their minds racing with questions about the child's identity and the circumstances that led to this tragic end.

Upon closer examination, the authorities noted several key details. The boy appeared to be between five and seven years old, standing less than four feet tall with blond hair and brown eyes. His physical condition suggested he was well-nourished, and there were no visible signs of abuse. However, it was evident he had been struck with a blunt instrument, and his body could have been in the water for several months.

What caught both the police and the public's attention was the boy's attire, which hinted at a more affluent background. He was dressed in a gray sweater from the prestigious Bradley Knitting Company, Munsing underwear, black stockings, a blouse, and patent leather shoes. The high quality of his clothing suggested he came from a well-to-do family, making the mystery of his death even more perplexing.

In a desperate bid to identify the boy, his body was displayed at a local funeral home, but no one came forward to claim him. The community was left with more questions than answers, and the boy was eventually buried on March 17, 1921, without his identity being uncovered.

The press, captivated by the tragic tale, began referring to the boy as "Little Lord Fauntleroy," a name inspired by a character from Frances Hodgson Burnett's beloved children's book. This character, known for his lavish dress and manners, seemed a fitting moniker for the mysterious child found in such fine clothing.

Despite extensive investigations and collaborations with the Milwaukee police department, the identity of Little Lord Fauntleroy remained elusive. The case captured national attention for a time, but ultimately, the story of the small boy found in the quarry pond faded into history, leaving behind a legacy of unanswered questions and haunting speculation.

## Investigation

An employee at the O'Laughlin Company recounted an unsettling encounter that occurred five weeks before the child's body was discovered. The employee remembered a couple approaching him on a seemingly ordinary day. The woman, wearing a striking red sweater, appeared visibly distressed and tearful as she inquired if he had seen a young boy in the vicinity. Her companion, a man, was observed intently watching the specific area where the child's body would later be found. After this brief and peculiar exchange, the couple left in a Ford vehicle and subsequently vanished without a trace.

A haunting theory emerged among investigators suggesting that Little Lord Fauntleroy might have been kidnapped from a wealthy family in a distant location. His body was possibly disposed of in Waukesha to obscure his identity and origins. Despite initial fervor, the investigation reached a standstill, and no new leads surfaced.

In the aftermath, a compassionate local woman named Minnie Conrad spearheaded a fundraising effort to give the child a proper burial. Thanks to her initiative, Little Lord Fauntleroy was laid to rest at Prairie Home Cemetery in Waukesha. In a poignant twist of fate, Minnie Conrad herself was buried in the same cemetery in 1940, passing away at the age of seventy-three.

Adding to the mystery, sightings of a woman shrouded in a heavy veil were reported. This enigmatic figure would occasionally place flowers on the boy's grave, sparking rumors and speculation. Some believed that this mysterious mourner might have known the true identity of Little

Lord Fauntleroy, forever connecting her to the unsolved tragedy.

**Foul Play Was Suspected**

Investigators faced a daunting challenge as they tried to determine how long the child had been submerged in the pond. Their estimates ranged wildly, from less than a week to as much as six months. The boy's attire suggested he came from a wealthy background, yet his identity remained a mystery to the police.

In a desperate bid for information, the authorities displayed the child, whom they had dubbed "Little Lord Fauntleroy," at a local funeral home. They invited the public to view the body, hoping someone might recognize him. Numerous groups came to see the child, but no one could provide any useful information—until a quarry worker named Mike Koker stepped forward.

Koker offered the first significant lead in the case. He recounted seeing a young woman in a red sweater wandering near the pond five weeks before the body was discovered. When he approached her and asked what she was doing, she seemed agitated and asked if he had seen a little boy in the area. Shortly after, she joined a male companion, and the two drove away in a car.

Despite extensive efforts, the couple was never found by the police. However, a tip led authorities to believe the woman had died by suicide in the same pond where the boy was found. They resorted to using dynamite in the water, hoping the explosion would bring another corpse to the surface. Unfortunately, their efforts yielded no additional bodies.

Detectives initially theorized that the couple might have sent the boy away temporarily while they were otherwise occupied, leading to an accidental drowning. However, the coroner's examination told a different story. The boy had a severe head injury, indicative of being struck by a blunt object. Additionally, he had very little water in his lungs, suggesting he was already dead before ending up in the pond.

These revelations pointed to a more sinister scenario, where the child was likely murdered and then disposed of in the water. The mystery of Little Lord Fauntleroy deepened, leaving both investigators and the community grappling for answers.

**The Investigation Grows Colder**

The search for answers grew more desperate as the days turned into weeks. The police took an aggressive approach, plastering the boy's image in every newspaper across the Midwest. Sheriff Keebler, C.A. Dean, and District Attorney Allen D. Young, determined to crack the case, initially offered a financial reward of $250 for any information that could unearth the boy's identity or lead to the capture of his killers. The silence was deafening. Raising the reward to $1,000 did nothing to break the wall of mystery surrounding the case.

Just when it seemed all hope was lost, a potential lead emerged. David Dobrick, the owner of the Liberty Department Store in Waukesha, contacted the police with a compelling claim. He was certain he had sold the clothes the boy, dubbed "Little Lord Fauntleroy," had been wearing during a January sale. Yet, without any records to trace the purchaser, this promising lead turned into a dead end.

Months passed, and another glimmer of hope appeared. A man from Chicago named J.B. Belson came forward, asserting that he knew the child's identity. Belson declared that the boy was his nephew, the son of his sister, Mrs. G.E. Hormidge. His sister's ex-husband had allegedly kidnapped their two children and made threats to kill them on numerous occasions. The story seemed plausible and gave the investigators a renewed sense of purpose.

However, after thoroughly investigating Belson's claim, the police discovered that the children were alive and well. The boy found in Waukesha was not Belson's nephew. This lead, like the others, crumbled under scrutiny, leaving the investigation at a standstill.

Realizing that the mystery might never be solved, Sheriff Keebler made the somber decision to lay Little Lord Fauntleroy to rest. The boy's remains were transported to the Weber Funeral Home for preparation. In a touching display of community solidarity, a local woman named Minnie Conrad spearheaded a fundraising effort to cover the funeral expenses.

On March 14, 1921, at precisely 2:00 PM, a small white casket was tenderly lowered into the earth at Prairie Home Cemetery. An unknown hand had lovingly inscribed "Our Darling" on the lid of the casket. For years to come, Minnie Conrad placed a bouquet on the boy's grave annually, honoring the memory of a child whose true identity remained shrouded in mystery until her own passing.

This heartbreaking tale of an unidentified boy, lost to time, resonates deeply and serves as a poignant reminder of the countless stories that remain untold, waiting to be uncovered.

**Homer Lemay Connection**

In the year 1949, an intriguing hypothesis emerged from Milwaukee, Wisconsin. Dr. E.L. Tharinger, a medical examiner, proposed a compelling theory regarding the identity of an unidentified boy whose body had been discovered decades earlier. He suggested that this unknown child might be Homer Lemay, a six-year-old boy who vanished under mysterious circumstances around the same time the unidentified boy was found.

Homer Lemay's disappearance was shrouded in ambiguity and conflicting accounts. According to his father, Edmond Lemay, Homer had been adopted by a Chicago couple known as the Nortons in 1921. Edmond claimed that the Nortons had taken Homer on a trip to South America, where a tragic accident occurred. He recounted that he had received a newspaper clipping from South America detailing an automobile accident that allegedly killed his son. However, this story raised more questions than it answered.

Investigators thoroughly examined Edmond Lemay's account but could not find any evidence to substantiate it. No records of the purported accident existed, nor could they verify the existence of the Nortons. This lack of evidence cast a shadow of doubt over Edmond's story, leading to more speculation about what truly happened to Homer Lemay.

In a significant development on May 16, 1949, Dr. Tharinger held a press conference urging the exhumation of the unidentified boy's remains. He believed that modern forensic techniques could potentially reveal whether the boy was indeed Homer Lemay. Dr. Tharinger publicly appealed to Sheriff Leslie P. Rock-teacher and Coroner Alvin H. Johnson to make the final decision on the exhumation. However, after much delib-eration, they decided against disturbing the boy's resting place, opting to leave the Little Lord Fauntleroy undisturbed.

Today, the unidentified boy lies in Prairie Home Cemetery in Waukesha, Wisconsin, under a simple tombstone that offers few clues to the enduring mystery surrounding him. The tombstone reads, "Unknown Boy Found in O'Laughlin Quarry. Waukesha, Wis. March 8, 1921." Despite numerous theories and investigations, the true identity of the boy remains unknown, leaving a poignant and unresolved chapter in true crime history.

The tale of Homer Lemay and the unidentified boy is a haunting reminder of the complexities and uncertainties that often accompany historical mysteries. While the passage of time has not yet yielded definitive answers, the dedication of individuals like Dr. Tharinger keeps the hope alive that one day, the truth may finally be uncovered. Until then, the Little Lord Fauntleroy remains a silent testament to a long-forgotten tragedy, waiting for the moment when his story will be fully told.

More than a century has passed, yet the enigma of Little Lord Fauntleroy lives on. This unresolved case remains a haunting reminder of the many puzzles that history conceals, urging us always to seek the truth, no matter how elusive it may seem.

The story of Little Lord Fauntleroy is not just a tale of a young boy whose life was tragically cut short; it symbolizes the enduring allure of historical mysteries and the human desire to understand the past. How could it be that this innocent child was murdered, and no one stepped forward to claim him? What circumstances led to his untimely death?

This perplexing narrative leaves us without answers, compelling us to grasp at the threads of history in an attempt to weave together the fabric of the past. The mystery of Little Lord Fauntleroy serves as a somber testament to the lengths that time can go to in order to shroud the truth. Yet, it also highlights our unyielding quest for knowledge and justice, even when the odds of resolution seem slim.

In reflecting on this case, we are reminded of the countless other stories that remain hidden in history, waiting for someone to unearth their secrets. The tale of Little Lord Fauntleroy is a call to all who are fascinated by the past to continue their pursuit of truth, driven by the hope that someday, we might finally piece together these age-old puzzles and bring closure to the mysteries that have long haunted our collective memory. We might never know what happened to this innocent little boy, but our pursuit of answers keeps his memory alive and underscores the importance of understanding our history, no matter how confusing it might be.

# CHAPTER SEVEN

## THE DISAPPEARANCE OF PAULINE PICARD

In the heart of Brittany, France, the Picard family lived a simple life on their farm in the quaint village of Goas al Ludu. It was the year 1922, a time when life for many was dictated by the rhythms of nature rather than the hustle and bustle of modernity. For the Picards, this idyllic existence was soon to be shattered by an episode that would reverberate through the pages of history, leaving behind a haunting mystery.

### A Fateful Spring Day

April 6, 1922, began like any other day for the Picard family. Two-year-old Pauline Picard was a bubbly toddler, full of life and wonder. She spent her days playing amidst the rolling fields and under the watchful eyes of her family. Yet, as the sun set that evening, the lively chatter around the dinner table turned to worried murmurs. Pauline was nowhere to be found.

The initial shock of her disappearance quickly turned into a frantic search. Her family, joined by over a hundred townspeople, scoured every inch of the farm and surrounding woods. The dense thickets were explored, every hollow and ditch examined. Despite their exhaustive efforts, not a single trace of the little girl was found. Whispers of foul play began to circulate, but without evidence, all they had were unsettling rumors.

**The Theories and Suspicions**

The weeks that followed were filled with anguish and uncertainty. Some suggested that Pauline had wandered off, succumbing to the elements or perhaps falling prey to a wild boar. Others recalled a chimney sweep who had been seen offering candy to children, while neighbors spoke of two mysterious figures loitering near the farm. Despite these suspicions, no concrete leads emerged.

The gendarmes and local police officers left no stone unturned. They questioned everyone in the village and even reached out to nearby towns. Yet, Pauline seemed to have vanished into thin air, leaving behind a heartbroken family and a community on edge.

Days turned into weeks, and whispers of grim theories filled the air. Some feared she had been kidnapped by roaming vagabonds, although no such group was known to be in the area around the time of her disappearance. The lack of evidence or sightings left everyone grasping at straws, hoping against hope for a breakthrough.

## A Shocking Twist

Just when hope seemed lost, an unexpected twist unfolded.

Amidst the cloud of despair enveloping the Picard family, a glimmer of hope emerged in May when the police brought forth a photograph of a little girl found wandering alone in Cherbourg, over two hundred miles away. The child had been discovered abandoned in a hallway on Rue Coypel, having been earlier spotted with a woman dressed in rags who attempted to desert her in a store.

When Pauline's mother saw the photograph, her heart leaped with a mix of hope and disbelief. "It is really my daughter," she cried. Overwhelmed by emotion and the possibility of reunion, the Picards embarked on their first-ever train journey to Cherbourg to reclaim their daughter.

Upon their arrival, the reunion was bittersweet. The girl, though strikingly similar to Pauline, remained mute and unresponsive to the Picards' joyous greetings. Her indifference and failure to understand their Breton language cast a shadow of doubt over their initial certainty. However, the prosecutor, hopeful for recovery through familiarity, entrusted the silent child to the Picards, who undertook the return journey with cautious optimism.

## A Return to Goas-al-Ludu

Back in Goas-al-Ludu, the girl believed to be Pauline was welcomed with tentative hope by the community. Her siblings recognized her, and even the family cat acknowledged her. Yet, despite fleeting signs of recognition, doubts lingered in the minds of those who knew Pauline best.

The mystery deepened when Yves Martin, a farmer with an earlier outburst of guilt, once again made his presence known. Upon his questioning of the girl's identity, his subsequent breakdown and commitment to an asylum fueled rumors and speculation about his possible involvement in Pauline's disappearance.

For a moment, it seemed as if the mystery of Pauline's disappearance had been resolved. However, fate had other plans.

**The Discovery of a Body**

Late May 1922, the quiet village was shaken by a discovery that would haunt its residents. The body of a young girl was found near the Picard family's farm, but the reports on the exact date and distance varied. According to Le Matin, a prominent publication from Brest, a cyclist stumbled upon the decomposing body on May 25, just over 3,000 feet from Goas-al-Ludu. In contrast, Le Petit Parisien reported it as May 26, with the distance being between 2,600 and 3,000 feet from the farm. Meanwhile, The New York Times stated that a farmer discovered the corpse one mile from the village on May 25.

Regardless of the discrepancies, what was undeniable was the horrific state in which the girl's body was found. Naked, decapitated, and missing her hands and feet, she lay in a ditch that had been meticulously searched during the initial days of her disappearance. The questions lingered—how could something so grisly have gone unnoticed?

Adding to the eerie scene was the presence of a man's skull nearby. It suggested that there might be another victim, though the identity remained a mystery; the face was unrecognizable, ravaged by foxes. Close to the girl's body, a pair of galoshes, socks, and a fustian dress were neatly folded. These bloodstained clothes were identified by the Picard family as belonging to their daughter, Pauline.

When the gendarmes arrived, accompanied by curious villagers, the Picards' hearts sank as they recognized the garments. Despite being unable to identify the corpse due to animal predation, François Picard initially affirmed that it was his daughter. However, when pressed by a commissioner from Rennes, doubt clouded his conviction. "It's her clothes," he said, "But is it her body? Oh! The other is so similar!"

Medical professionals were called in to examine the body, yet the findings only deepened the mystery. Dr. Pouliquen identified wounds and dispatched the body to Châteaulin for further study. Dr. Gouriou's subsequent examination uncovered a stab wound in the groin area. Even with this evidence of violent trauma, some investigators speculated that exposure might have been the cause of death. The autopsy, unfortunately, yielded no decisive conclusions.

The girl's torso and stomach remained untouched by scavengers, though these are usually the first parts to be consumed. This peculiar detail left investigators puzzled. Did she die from starvation, or was she held captive, deprived of food by her captors?

The village of Goas-al-Ludu was left with many questions. How could such a heinous act occur unnoticed? Who was the man whose skull lay beside her? And, most haunting of all, if this was not Pauline, then where was she?

**The Suspects Emerge**

In any investigation, suspicion often casts a wide net. In Pauline's case, the gaze of suspicion fell heavily upon Christophe Kéramon, an itinerant umbrella peddler and occasional agricultural worker for the Picards. Known for his past criminal record—a five-year imprisonment for rape—Kéramon's presence in the village on the day of Pauline's disappearance did not go unnoticed. Witnesses recalled how he had been particularly attentive to Pauline during his visit, even overhearing him promising her a better home elsewhere.

Despite Kéramon's suspicious behavior, François Picard provided an alibi that placed him miles away from Goas-al-Ludu when Pauline vanished. Arrested briefly for not carrying his internal passport, Kéramon was ultimately released after serving a month for unrelated charges. The shadow of doubt lingered but without concrete evidence, the authorities had no choice but to set him free.

Yves Martin, a middle-aged farmer, added another layer of intrigue to the case. Upon visiting the Picard home and learning of their daughter's supposed return, Martin's peculiar reaction raised eyebrows. He questioned whether they were certain it was Pauline and, in a fit of hysteria, declared his guilt before fleeing. The following day, Martin was committed to a psychiatric hospital, leaving behind a trail of unanswered questions.

## The Lingering Mystery

When the Châteaulinois judge declared the lifeless body found to be that of the missing Pauline Picard, the community was left in shock. Her death was ruled accidental, and she was laid to rest in Saint-Rivoal. The coffin was simple, crafted from white wood, symbolizing the innocence of a life cut tragically short. But just as the soil settled on her grave, whispers began to ripple through the cobblestone streets and lush fields of Brittany.

By June 1922, a rumor emerged—Pauline Picard might not be resting in peace after all. Instead, tales circulated that she had been spirited away by a wealthy family, eager to conceal the unfortunate demise of their own child. These rumors hinted at a dark conspiracy, the exchange of one life for another, with an innocent girl trapped in a life not her own. This chilling possibility was enough to capture the attention of the nation.

The renowned French newspaper Le Petit Parisien speculated that this gossip might lead to a reopening of the investigation. The notion that the body identified as Pauline's could belong to someone else, perhaps even a child from a well-to-do family, was tantalizing. Yet, even as the rumors intensified, the legal system remained silent, and no new inquiries were launched.

Fast forward to October 2017, and the advances in forensic science brought renewed hope for answers. However, no genetic testing had been conducted on the remains buried under Pauline's name. The mystery lingered, unsolved and unsettling. Was it truly Pauline who lay in that white coffin, or had her identity been mistaken, her fate left hanging in the balance of time and speculation?

The Cherbourg girl, initially thought to be the vanished child, was returned to her city on June 13, 1922. But despite the official declarations that identified her as someone else, the mystery did not lay to rest. Whispers of darker forces and hidden truths circulated among the public and press alike. Was there a conspiracy woven into the fabric of this tragic story? Did the truth lie buried, much like the child herself?

Almost two months after her return, the girl began speaking fluent Breton, a remarkable development that led the popular newspaper Le Petit Parisien to boldly assert that she was indeed the real Pauline Picard. The mystery deepened with each passing day, capturing the imaginations of families who were eager to adopt "the girl with the pretty smile," as she became fondly known.

She took on a new identity, Marie-Louise Pauline, bestowed upon her by the civil court of Cherbourg. Her days were spent under the care of the Franciscan Sisters of Notre-Dame-du-Vœu, yet her life was tragically cut short by measles in early 1924, casting another dark shadow over the Picard family saga—a story already steeped in sorrow.

The story of Pauline Picard continues to leave an indelible mark on all who hear it—a vivid reminder of innocence lost and the relentless pursuit of truth by those left behind. Her tale weaves itself into the expansive tapestry of true crime, resonating like a poignant enigma that speaks to our deepest fears and the lengths we go to seeking answers, even when they elude us.

# CHAPTER EIGHT

## THE TEXARKANA MOONLIGHT MURDERS

In the ominous shadows of 1946, the Texarkana Moonlight Murders cast a pall over a small American community nestled along the Arkansas-Texas border. Dubbed by the press as the work of "The Phantom Killer," these chilling events left an indelible mark on the psyche of the nation. Over the course of ten terrifying weeks, an unidentified predator wrought havoc, leaving a trail of blood and fear in his wake.

The Phantom's reign of terror began on February 22 and lasted until May 3, targeting unsuspecting young couples seeking solace in the privacy of lovers' lanes or secluded country roads. Under the cloak of darkness, the killer struck with methodical precision, his violent spree culminating in eight victims—five of whom perished in the moonlit carnage. The final brutal assault occurred not on a deserted road, but within the supposed safety of an isolated Arkansas farmhouse, shattering any illusions of security.

Word of these gruesome crimes rapidly spread beyond Texarkana's borders, capturing national and international attention. The community, gripped by panic, transformed into a fortress of mistrust. Residents armed themselves, retreating indoors at dusk while law enforcement officers diligently patrolled the now-empty streets. Hardware stores saw their shelves emptied of guns, ammunition, and locks as fear morphed into a tangible presence.

## The Crimes

Four savage attacks unraveled under the cloak of night, each meticulously timed to strike terror into the hearts of unsuspecting couples. These assaults, occurring during weekend nights when the allure of solitude was at its peak, targeted heterosexual pairs seeking secluded spots away from prying eyes. The meticulous pattern of the attacks, with a chilling regularity of three to four weeks between each incident, suggested a calculated cruelty that left the community on edge.

### February 22: The First Attack: The Haunting Night

In the still of the night on February 22, 1946, a chilling encounter unfolded that would mark the beginning of a series of terrifying events in Texarkana. At around 11:45 p.m., Jimmy Hollis, a 25-year-old local, and his 19-year-old girlfriend, Mary Jeanne Larey, found themselves parked on a desolate road, seeking a moment of intimacy after an evening at the movies. This isolated lovers' lane, merely 300 feet from the nearest city homes where today's Central Mall stands, became the stage for an unexpected horror.

Just ten minutes into their private interlude, a shadowy figure emerged from the darkness. The assailant, concealed behind a makeshift mask fashioned from a white cloth with crudely cut eyeholes, suddenly appeared at the driver's side window. With a flashlight casting blinding beams into the car's interior, the ominous figure shattered the tranquility. Jimmy attempted to reason with him, asserting he must have them mistaken for someone else. Yet, the man's chilling response was unforgettable, "I don't want to kill you, fellow, so do what I say."

Both Hollis and Larey were coerced out of the car, the tension palpable in the night air. The masked man turned his attention to Hollis with a disturbing command to "take off his goddamn britches." Compliance brought no mercy; the gun-wielding figure struck Hollis twice on the head. The impact was so fierce that Larey initially believed gunshots had fired, but it was the gruesome sound of Hollis's skull cracking.

In a desperate bid to placate their attacker, Larey offered Hollis's wallet, hoping to convince him of their lack of money. Instead, she was met with violence, struck down with a blunt instrument. The assailant then ordered her to run. Confused and terrified, Larey first moved toward a nearby ditch but was redirected by the attacker to flee up the road.

Stumbling upon an old, abandoned car, Larey hoped for refuge but found it empty. Her attempts to escape were thwarted when the assailant reappeared, questioning her actions. Accusing her of deceit, he brutally knocked her down, subjecting her to a horrifying assault using the barrel of his gun. In the throes of terror and pain, Larey managed to break free, sprinting half a mile to safety.

Reaching a nearby home, Larey desperately roused the residents and contacted the police, her voice filled with the urgency of survival. Meanwhile, Hollis, having regained consciousness, flagged down a passing motorist who also alerted law enforcement. Within half an hour, Sheriff W. H. "Bill" Presley and his team arrived at the scene, but the predator had vanished into the shadows.

Larey was treated overnight for a head wound, while Hollis endured several days in the hospital, recovering from severe skull fractures. Their accounts of the attacker diverged—Larey believed the assailant to be a light-skinned African-American male, whereas Hollis recalled a tanned white man around thirty years old. Despite their discrepancies, both agreed the figure stood about 6 feet tall. Skepticism surrounded Larey's account, with law enforcement suspecting the pair might know more about their attacker than they were willing to reveal.

### March 24th: The First Double Murder

In the quiet, early hours of Sunday, March 24th, 1946, a grim discovery was made on a secluded lovers' lane just off US Highway 67 West in Bowie County. A passing motorist stumbled upon a scene that would soon become infamous—a double murder that would haunt the local community and puzzle investigators for years to come.

Richard Griffin, a 29-year-old with a promising future, and Polly Ann Moore, his 17-year-old girlfriend of just six weeks, were found lifeless in Griffin's parked car. The vehicle, a silent witness to the night's horrors, sat eerily still, 100 yards from the main highway.

Griffin's body was discovered in a peculiar position. He was on his knees between the front seats, his head resting solemnly on his crossed hands, as if he had been praying. His pockets had been turned inside out, suggesting a possible robbery. In the back seat, Polly Ann Moore lay face-down, her life cut tragically short. Investigators speculated that her body had been moved to the back seat after she was killed outside the car, possibly placed there on a blanket.

The evidence suggested a chilling sequence of events. Griffin had been shot twice while seated in the car, with both he and Moore suffering a single gunshot wound to the back of the head. Despite being fully clothed, their deaths displayed a level of brutality that sent shivers down the spines of those who arrived first on the scene. A blood-soaked patch of earth near the car indicated that at least part of the grim act occurred outside the vehicle, with congealed blood on the running board painting a macabre picture of violence on that fateful night.

A .32 caliber cartridge casing was recovered, hinting at the murder weapon—a pistol likely wrapped in a blanket to muffle the shots. Yet, despite the clues left behind, no formal examination by a pathologist was recorded for either victim, leaving many questions unanswered.

Local rumors at the time whispered of a possible sexual assault on Polly Ann Moore, adding an additional layer of horror to the crime, but modern accounts have refuted these claims. The lack of clear forensic evidence left the double murder shrouded in mystery, fueling speculation and fear among the residents of Bowie County.

This chilling event marked the beginning of a series of crimes that would become known as the Texarkana Moonlight Murders, etching the tale of Richard Griffin and Polly Ann Moore into the pages of true crime history.

### April 14: The Second Double-Murder

In the sunlit corners of Texarkana, shadows of fear began to creep in, and the murmur of another unsolved enigma fluttered through the tight-knit community.

In the early hours of Sunday, April 14, 1946, Paul Martin, a vibrant 17-year-old, picked up his friend Betty Jo Booker, 15, from her spirited musical gig at the VFW Club on West Fourth and Oak Street. Little did they know, these would be the last moments they would share in the safety of the night's quiet.

By 6:30 a.m., a harrowing discovery was made. The lifeless body of Martin lay forlornly on its left side at the edge of North Park Road. The scene was gruesome and perplexing, with blood splattered across the road by a nearby fence. He bore the marks of a brutal attack, having been shot four times in a calculated manner—through the nose, into the ribs from behind, in the right hand, and a final devastating shot through the back of his neck.

Hours later, as the sun mounted higher into the sky, a search party stumbled upon Booker's body at approximately 11:30 a.m., nestled nearly two miles away from where Martin had been found. Her body was positioned carefully, lying on her back behind a tree, fully clothed but eerily posed with her right hand tucked into the pocket of her overcoat. The young girl had suffered two gunshot wounds—one piercing her chest, the other marring her youthful face. The chilling revelation that the same .32 automatic Colt pistol had been used in both her murder and an earlier double-homicide only deepened the mystery.

Martin's vehicle was discovered roughly three miles from Booker's resting place and about 1.55 miles from where his own body was found. It was parked with an unsettling nonchalance outside Spring Lake Park, the keys still dangling in the ignition. Despite thorough investigations, authorities found themselves tangled in a web of uncertainty, unable to determine which victim had faced the killer's wrath first.

Texas Ranger Manuel T. Gonzaullas, alongside Presley, scrutinized the evidence, noting that both Paul and Betty Jo seemed to have fought fiercely against their attacker. Yet, according to Tom Albritton, Martin's close friend, no signs indicated a quarrel had occurred between the victims, nor did Martin have known enemies.

In a town gripped by terror and suspicion, the brutal slayings of Paul Martin and Betty Jo Booker added another chapter to the dark saga that haunted Texarkana—an unsolved puzzle that would confound both authorities and residents alike.

### May 3: The Fifth Murder

On a seemingly ordinary Friday night, May 3rd, the tranquility of a rural farmhouse would be shattered by an act of cold-blooded violence that sent further ripples of fear across the Texarkana region. Nestled on a sprawling 500-acre farm off Highway 67 East, nearly ten miles northeast of Texarkana, Virgil Starks, 37, settled into an armchair with the evening newspaper. The comfort of his home would soon be pierced by two bullets fired through a closed double window, striking Virgil in the back of his head.

The sound of breaking glass set off a chain of events that seemed almost surreal. Katie Starks, Virgil's 36-year-old wife, rushed from another room, her eyes meeting the horrific scene of Virgil struggling to rise, only to collapse back into his chair, the life ebbing from him. In the grip of shock and fear, Katie raced to the crank telephone, desperate to summon help. But as she dialed twice, two gunshots from the same window found their mark, hitting her in the face.

Despite the searing pain and the blinding haze of her own blood, Katie's will to survive propelled her into action. She stumbled through the house, hoping to retrieve a pistol but was forced to abandon her plan when she heard the ominous presence of the killer at the back of the house. Barefoot and bleeding, Katie fled through the front door, the cool night air a stark contrast to the chaos she left behind.

Her escape led her across the road, seeking refuge at the home of her sister and brother-in-law. Finding their house empty, she pressed on to the nearby residence of A. V. Prater. Breathless and battered, she managed to utter, "Virgil's dead," before succumbing to exhaustion and collapsing. Prater, quick to act, fired a rifle into the night sky, a desperate signal for help that reached the ears of neighbor Elmer Taylor. Responding to Prater's call, Taylor retrieved his car, and together with other members of the Prater family, they transported Katie to Michael Meagher Hospital—today known as the Miller County Health Unit.

In the operating room, Katie was met by Miller County Sheriff W. E. Davis, who had taken the lead on the investigation. Her testimony, given while she lay wounded, added flesh to a harrowing narrative that had begun to take shape. Just four days later, in a follow-up conversation with Sheriff Davis, Katie squashed a burgeoning rumor suggesting Virgil had been on edge, hearing a car lurking outside their home night after night, haunted by the sense that death was approaching.

The events of that night painted a chilling portrait of terror, a vivid reminder of the fragility of safety and the indomitable will to survive even in the face of relentless horror.

### Unraveling the Mystery: Investigations Intensify

The atmosphere in Texarkana was thick with tension as law enforcement grappled with unraveling the twisted threads of a chilling series of attacks. The first incident, involving Larey and Hollis, left investigators dubious about their account. Larey's insistence that she had no knowledge of the assailant's identity fell on skeptical ears, with authorities suspecting a cover-up. Despite the pressure, Larey returned to town after the brutal Griffin-Moore murders, hoping to connect the dots and identify the shadowy figure who haunted the community. Yet, the

Texas Rangers remained unconvinced, pressing her for details they believed she withheld.

Only after the Texarkana Gazette interviewed Larey did officials break their silence, urging citizens to report anyone whose whereabouts were suspiciously unaccounted for during the murder spree. This call to action signaled a turning point in the investigation, igniting public awareness and cooperation.

### A City on Edge

The brutal slayings of Griffin and Moore triggered an all-out, citywide investigative assault. Local law enforcement joined forces with the Texas and Arkansas police, the Texas Department of Public Safety, FBI, and various sheriff's departments, in an unprecedented collaborative effort. Over 200 individuals were interrogated, and a slew of false leads pursued, each one a potential key to unlocking the mystery.

In the wake of the Martin-Booker case, detectives doggedly pursued every lead, interrogating acquaintances and suspects around the clock. Gonzaullas, a seasoned investigator, devised a risky tactic—using teenagers as bait in parked cars, officers lying in wait nearby. Even law enforcement officers took on the role of decoys, some using mannequins or real partners to lure the perpetrator into a trap.

Following the grisly attack of the Starks couple, reinforcements from surrounding areas flooded Texarkana. Roadblocks sprang up on Highway 67 East, and anyone near the scene during the time of the murder found themselves in custody for questioning. By early May, a formidable task force of 47 officers worked tirelessly to crack the case, bolstered by the arrival of a mobile radio station and a fleet of prowl cars from the Arkansas State Police.

Despite their efforts, the investigation seemed to stall, with no clear motive emerging. Theories swirled, with a disturbing consensus forming around the idea of a "sex maniac," particularly since significant sums of money and personal belongings were left untouched at the crime scenes.

By March's end, authorities offered a $500 reward for information, a sum that quickly ballooned as fear and desperation gripped the community. The Booker-Martin murders spurred the reward to surpass $10,000—a testament to the community's desperation for resolution and justice. Skepticism persisted regarding any connection between the Starks' case and previous crimes, largely due to the varying caliber of weaponry suspected in each attack.

By late 1948, the trail grew cold, and investigators began to distance the Starks case from the earlier double murders. Yet, questions lingered, whispering through the corridors of Texarkana—a town forever changed by the specter of its unsolved mysteries.

**Public Reaction**

The Griffin-Moore murders, while unsettling, were initially perceived as isolated acts of violence. Officials remained tight-lipped about any connection to the earlier Hollis-Larey attack, keeping the community unaware of a potentially sinister pattern. However, the brutal slaying of

Martin and Booker signaled a chilling possibility—a serial predator was on the loose. These tragic deaths reverberated through Texarkana, where the tight-knit community was left reeling.

Polly Booker wasn't just any victim; she was a beacon of promise—a high-school junior adored by her peers, a sorority member, a band officer, and a decorated scholar and musician. Her tragic end prompted an overwhelming response from her high school, which curtailed classes to allow hundreds of students to pay their respects at her funeral. Businesses imposed curfews, and the streets, once bustling after dark, fell eerily silent.

It was in this tense atmosphere that local media christened the unknown assailant "The Phantom Killer." The moniker echoed through the public consciousness, as fear took hold. That fear escalated into full-blown panic following the savage murder of Virgil Starks in his own home. Newspapers like the Texarkana Gazette warned that the killer could strike again at any time, fueling paranoia. Reports of prowlers flooded police stations as citizens' imaginations ran wild, driven by terror and the relentless coverage.

Texarkana's residents, who once left doors unlocked without a second thought, now fortified their homes. Locks, firearms, ammunition, and even Venetian blinds flew off the shelves. People armed themselves with guns, nailed shut windows, and shielded their homes with every imaginable protective device. The day after Starks's death, stores sold out of security essentials, from night latches to window guards.

With nerves frayed and firearms at the ready, Texarkana teetered on the brink of chaos. Law enforcement officers, aware of the hair-trigger fear gripping the town, approached homes with caution—sirens blaring, headlights illuminating their approach, vocally identifying themselves to avoid startling armed homeowners.

The terror wasn't confined to Texarkana alone. The ripple effect spread to towns like Hope, Lufkin, and Magnolia, even reaching as far as Oklahoma City, where surges in gun and axe purchases were recorded. For three weeks, no further killings occurred, and the palpable tension began to ease. By summer's end, the collective anxiety started to wane, but the memory of those dark days lingered, etched into the fabric of the community.

**Rumors**

In the tense atmosphere that gripped the town, whispers quickly turned into a cacophony of rumors, heightening the sense of paranoia and complicating the police's pursuit for justice. On April 18, Gonzaullas, with an air of urgency, convened a press conference to address the swirling whirlwind of misinformation. His words were direct and imposing; he categorically denied any capture of the elusive murderer. "The rumors circulating both among the public and within the pages of newspapers," he declared, "are not just a mere distraction; they are a direct impediment to our investigation and pose a risk to innocent lives."

This message was reinforced in a gripping radio interview on May 7, where Gonzaullas's voice resonated through the airwaves, imploring, "These rumors divert our officers from the true path of our investigation. Capturing this man is of utmost importance, and we cannot afford to dismiss any lead, no matter how extraordinary it appears."

Yet, despite these stern warnings, speculation continued to surge through the town like an unstoppable tide. By mid-May, many locals were convinced that the murderer had been apprehended, with some spinning tales of his secretive detention at the Bowie County Jail or his covert transfer to another location. The Gazette and News offices became inundated with a barrage of calls—both from nearby and distant locales—seeking confirmation of these allegations.

Amid this chaos, Presley stepped forward to address the community's fervor. With a plea for calm and rationality, he urged residents to demonstrate compassion and restraint, reminding them that baseless accusations could unfairly tarnish the reputations of innocent people suspected of being the Phantom. His call for empathy was a poignant reminder of the human cost of unchecked hysteria.

**Vigilantism in Texarkana**

Amidst the shadow of fear cast by the Phantom Killer, a palpable tension gripped the town of Texarkana. Yet, in defiance of palpable dread, some daring youths took to the deserted roads, fueled by a precarious mix of bravery and recklessness, hoping to unmask the elusive criminal themselves.

One night, Officer Johnson, accompanied by an Arkansas State Trooper, patrolled a particularly desolate stretch of road. Their headlights sliced through the darkness, revealing a lone vehicle parked ominously by the side. Johnson approached cautiously, his heart pounding with the anticipation of the unknown. Inside the car sat a young couple, seemingly unfazed by the terror lingering in the air.

With a nod, Johnson introduced himself, inquiring if they weren't afraid in such a vulnerable spot. The young woman's response was chillingly unexpected. With a steady hand, she revealed a .25 ACP pistol, pointed directly at him. "It's a good thing you told me who you are," she remarked, her voice carrying both relief and the steely resolve of someone ready to defend herself at all costs.

Meanwhile, on a different night, Texarkana City Police officers found themselves embroiled in a high-stakes chase after receiving reports of a suspicious car tailing a bus. The pursuit stretched across three miles, adrenaline coursing through their veins as they closed in on their target. The officers, driving an unmarked vehicle, finally brought their quarry to a halt by shooting out its tires, cornering a bewildered C. J. Lauderdale Jr.

Lauderdale, a local high-school athlete, sat wide-eyed in the station, confusion etched on his face. His explanation was simple yet unnerving; he claimed ignorance of the police presence, having followed the bus out of sheer suspicion of a mysterious passenger. This incident served as a stark reminder of the paranoia seeping into the town's fabric, where even innocent intentions could be misconstrued in the climate of fear.

On May 12, Captain Gonzaullas issued a stern warning in the Gazette, addressing the burgeoning group of "teenage sleuths". "It's a good way to get killed." His words hung heavy in the air, a sobering reminder of the dangers lurking in the shadows, where the lines between vigilante justice and perilous folly blurred alarmingly.

### The Phantom Killer

The enigmatic figure behind the Texarkana murders was not given a moniker until the tragic deaths of Booker and Martin. It was only after these grim events that the local media started dubbing him "The Phantom Killer." The April 16 issue of the Texarkana Daily News proclaimed, "Phantom Killer Eludes Officers as Investigation of Slayings Pressed." This gripping headline continued onto page two with the words, "Phantom Slayer Eludes Police." The next day, the Texarkana Gazette echoed this sentiment with its own chilling header, "Phantom Slayer Still at Large as Probe Continues." In 1946, J. Q. Mahaffey, the executive editor of the Gazette, recounted how Calvin Sutton, the managing editor, had an instinct for the dramatic. Sutton suggested they name the unknown murderer "The Phantom." Mahaffey agreed, quipping, "Why not? If this SOB keeps slipping through our fingers, he's earned that title!"

### Description of the Killer

Only Jimmy Hollis and Mary Jeanne Larey survived encounters with the Phantom to provide any description of the elusive attacker. They recalled a man standing six feet tall, his face obscured by a white mask with crude holes cut for his eyes and mouth—a specter of terror. Hollis guessed he was a young, dark-tanned Caucasian man under 30, while Larey believed he might be a light-skinned African American. With such contrasting accounts and no further descriptions from other attacks, it remains uncertain whether these atrocities were the handiwork of a singular monster or multiple perpetrators. Yet, the prevailing belief is that they were linked by a single, sinister presence.

**Modus Operandi of Terror**

The Phantom's signature style involved targeting young couples in secluded spots just beyond the city limits. Armed with a .32 caliber gun, he struck terror into the hearts of the community. Although the Starks murder deviated with a .22, most lawmen adhered to the belief that the Phantom wielded a .32. His pattern was consistent —he struck under the cloak of night on weekends, with eerie pauses of approximately three weeks between his attacks.

Captain Gonzaullas described the elusive murderer as a "shrewd criminal who had left no stone unturned to conceal his identity and activities," a mastermind whose trickery both confounded and frustrated law enforcement. At the Starks crime scene, Sheriff Presley remarked, "This killer is the luckiest person I have ever known. No one sees him, hears him in time, or can identify him in any way." Survivors and police alike agreed that the killer was a maniac with an unsettling expertise with firearms. Jimmy Hollis, a victim turned survivor, asserted, "I know he's crazy. The crazy things he said made me feel that his mind was warped."

Dr. Anthony Lapalla, a psychologist at the Federal Correctional Institution in Texarkana, theorized that the Phantom Killer was likely between his mid-30s and 50, driven by a potent blend of sexual compulsion and sadistic pleasure.

He believed the killer was highly intelligent and cunning, traits that often kept him out of the grasp of justice. Lapalla posited that the murderer was undeterred by police presence, choosing instead to adapt and shift his focus to more isolated targets, like the farmhouse attack on Virgil Starks. Despite his familiarity with the area, Lapalla speculated that the killer might not be a local resident, and certainly not a veteran, as he was living what appeared to be a normal life. The psychologist surmised the killer acted alone, keeping his dark deeds secret, with the potential to either continue his spree in a new locale or suppress the urge to kill. Lapalla concluded that this level of sophistication was unlikely in a black criminal, reflecting the prejudices of the era.

This chilling profile painted a picture of a ghostly figure, lurking in the shadows, ready to strike without warning—a true phantom haunting the lives of those in Texarkana.

**Suspects**

Throughout the tumultuous investigations of the infamous Phantom Killer case, nearly 400 individuals fell under the scrutinizing gaze of law enforcement. The case was rife with mystery and intrigue, where truth was tangled in a web of deception and false confessions. Tackett, a key investigator, recalled nine individuals who claimed to be the Phantom, but their tales unraveled in the face of hard facts. In the case of Hollis and Larey, the police found themselves chasing shadows, with no suspects apprehended. Yet, the Griffin and Moore investigation saw over 200 people questioned, along with a similar number of misleading tips and leads meticulously examined. Three individuals were initially detained for possession of blood-stained clothing; two walked free after providing plausible explanations. The third lingered in custody in Vernon, Texas, but was ultimately cleared of suspicion.

- **Youell Swinney**: A 29-year-old known for his life of crime as a car thief and counterfeiter. Arrested by Tackett in July for car thefts, Swinney's shadow loomed large on the night of the Griffin-Moore murders. His wife, Peggy, found herself in a web of confession and contradiction. She detailed Swinney's acts as the Phantom Killer, weaving a story that seemed to unravel with every iteration. Police confirmed some details, such as discarded possessions of the victims, lending weight to her words. Yet, Peggy's recantation rendered her an unreliable witness, unable to testify against her husband. For six months, law enforcement doggedly pursued the truth of Peggy's claims. However, evidence placed the Swinneys sleeping in their car near San Antonio on the night of the Booker-Martin slayings. Swinney, though never charged with murder, faced justice as a habitual offender for car theft. Rumors of a plea bargain lingered, suggesting Swinney's deep-rooted fear of a death sentence compelled him to accept his fate.
- **"Doodie" Tennison**: The enigmatic Henry Booker "Doodie" Tennison, an 18-year-old university freshman, left the world with a cryptic puzzle. On November 4, 1948, Tennison's suicide note implicated him in the murders of Booker, Martin, and Starks. A trombone player in Booker's high school band, Tennison's confession was a

tantalizing lead, yet no tangible evidence linked him to the crimes. An alibi from a friend cast further doubt, as they were together when news of the Starks murder broke.

- **Ralph Baumann**: A 21-year-old former Army Air Force machine-gunner, emerged from a fugue state to find his rifle missing. His tale of self-doubt and flight to Los Angeles painted him as a suspect in his own mind. Arrested for his confessions, Baumann's account crumbled under scrutiny. Discharged from the AAF as psychoneurotic, his claim of killing three people in Texarkana conflicted with established timelines.
- **Saxophone Peddler**: In a twist worthy of the noir novels of the era, investigators pinned hopes on Booker's missing saxophone as a lead. April 27 saw the arrest of a suspicious man in Corpus Christi, Texas, attempting to sell a saxophone. His evasiveness and flight raised alarms, yet no saxophone was found. Instead, a bag of bloody clothes in his hotel room deepened the intrigue. After exhaustive questioning, he was cleared, and Booker's saxophone emerged from its hiding place in the underbrush six months later.
- **German Prisoner of War**: The specter of an escaped German prisoner of war haunted the investigation. This stocky 24-year-old, having stolen a car in Arkansas and sought ammunition in Oklahoma, vanished like smoke. Authorities pursued him desperately, but his trail went cold, leaving questions unanswered.
- **Unknown Hitchhiker**: May 7 brought the chilling tale of a hitchhiker with a pistol, who carjacked

and robbed a man, boldly claiming responsibility for the Texarkana murders. Despite his frightening boasts, law enforcement remained skeptical, noting the killer's penchant for anonymity clashed with the hitchhiker's brashness.

- **Atoka County Suspect**: In Atoka, Oklahoma, a man's violent outburst and threats of murder led to a large-scale manhunt. Though apprehended, he was dismissed as the Phantom Killer when his alibi proved solid for the night of the Starks murder.
- **Sammie**: A local with a pristine reputation—until his vehicle's tire tracks appeared near Martin's body. Failing a polygraph test, Sammie's truth emerged under hypnosis, revealing a clandestine affair. Cleared by corroborated details, his secret remained buried with the case.
- **Earl McSpadden**: On May 7, as dawn broke over Texarkana, the mutilated body of Earl Cliff McSpadden was discovered on the railway tracks. Speculation flourished—was this the Phantom's final act, or had McSpadden ended his life, plagued by guilt? The coroner's ambiguous verdict fueled rumors that persisted long after the Phantom's shadow faded from Texarkana.

---

The Texarkana Moonlight Murders remain one of the most perplexing mysteries in American criminal history, characterized by a series of suspects whose connections to the heinous crimes were ultimately tenuous at best. Despite extensive investigations and numerous theories, the truth behind the Phantom Killer's identity and motives continues to elude law enforcement and the public alike. The case serves as a haunting reminder of the complexities and challenges of criminal investigations, leaving a lasting impact on the Texarkana community and the annals of true crime. As the shadows of suspicion linger, the quest for justice remains unfulfilled, compelling us to reflect on the nature of crime, fear, and the human experience.

# LISTEN TO THE PODCAST

APPLE PODCAST:
https://podcasts.apple.com/us/podcast/true-crime-sleep-stories/id1649396201

SPOTIFY:
https://open.spotify.com/show/3qDUjSgEY2T6KMHrFoLTaQ

YOUTUBE CHANNEL:
https://www.youtube.com/@TrueCrimeSleepStoriesPodcast

# CHAPTER NINE

## THE LADY OF THE DUNES

The chilling case of Ruth Marie Terry, better known as "The Lady of the Dunes," is one that has intrigued and mystified true crime followers for decades. Born on September 8, 1936, Terry's life was tragically cut short in what became a long-unsolved murder mystery until recent developments shed light on her story.

On a fateful day in the summer of 1974, the peaceful sands of Race Point Dunes near Provincetown, Massachusetts, became the site of a gruesome discovery. It was July 26 when Terry's body was found, and the scene was a haunting one. The dunes, typically alive with whispers of the ocean breeze, now held secrets of a violent past. Investigators determined that Terry had met a brutal end from a blow to the head. Her hands were missing, likely taken by her assailant to prevent identification through fingerprints. Even more chilling, her head was nearly severed, an indication of the violence she endured.

Despite the efforts to uncover her identity, Terry remained nameless for decades. Her body was exhumed multiple times—in 1980, 2000, and 2013—as authorities sought new clues using advancing forensic technologies. Each exhumation brought hope that her story would finally be told and justice served.

The breakthrough came on October 31, 2022, when the Boston FBI field office announced that the Lady of the Dunes had a name once more. Ruth Marie Terry's identity was confirmed, unraveling one piece of the mystery that had captivated investigators and the public alike. Yet, the question of who was responsible for her death lingered until August 28, 2023. It was then revealed that her husband, Guy Muldavin, who had died in 2002, was her killer. This revelation closed a nearly 50-year chapter of unanswered questions, but not without leaving a trail of sorrow and reflection on the violence she suffered.

---

Ruth Marie Terry's story begins in the humble setting of a mountainside shack in Whitwell, Tennessee. Born on September 8, 1936, to Johnny and Eva Terry, her early life was marked by hardship. Tragedy struck early with the death of her mother, Eva, at just 23, leaving a young Ruth to face the challenges of life with a sense of resilience.

By 1957, Ruth had experienced a brief marriage that ended as quickly as it began. Seeking new opportunities, she left her hometown for Livonia, Michigan, where she found work at the Fisher Body automotive plant. Just a year later, in 1958, she welcomed her son, Richard, into the world. However, the joy of motherhood was overshadowed by financial struggles. In a heartbreaking decision, Ruth arranged for her son to be adopted by Richard Hanchett Sr., her workplace superintendent, in exchange for settling her debts. This difficult choice marked a turning point in her life, leading her to leave Livonia for a fresh start in California.

Years passed, and in 1972, Ruth attempted to reconnect with her son. Unfortunately, the reunion was thwarted by a personal tragedy as Richard had suffered a drug overdose, resulting in an 18-day coma. The timing was obviously not right for them to meet, adding another layer of sorrow to Ruth's already complex life.

In 1974, Ruth married Guy Rockwell Muldavin, an antiques dealer, in Reno, Nevada. Their union was fraught with tension, as noted by Ruth's grandniece, Brittanie Novonglosky. She recalled how Ruth seemed to change around Muldavin, describing his behavior as possessive and controlling. This shift in Ruth's demeanor was further observed during a visit to her family in Whitwell just months before her untimely death.

Following their visit to Whitwell, Ruth and Muldavin traveled to Chattanooga, where they spent time with her half-brother Kenneth and his wife, Carole. The couple spoke of a grand adventure across the U.S., hunting for antiques. Massachusetts was one of the destinations mentioned, hinting at future plans that would never come to fruition.

The late summer of 1974 brought unsettling news. Muldavin returned to Tennessee alone, informing Ruth's family that she had vanished from their California home. His explanation was vague, claiming ignorance of her whereabouts. Concerned, Ruth's brother James took it upon himself to search for answers, traveling to California and hiring a private investigator. The investigator's findings were both baffling and disheartening. Ruth's possessions had been sold, and she was said to have left willingly, supposedly joining a religious cult.

For two decades, Ruth remained a mystery, her name appearing in family obituaries as deceased. Carole, her sister-in-law, speculated that perhaps Ruth was in witness protection, unable to reach out to her loved ones. These theories and unanswered questions clouded the truth of what really happened to Ruth Marie Terry, deepening the intrigue surrounding "The Lady of The Dunes."

**Discovery in the Dunes**

It was a summer day like any other on July 26, 1974, when a young girl's playful exploration turned into a haunting discovery. In the sunlit Race Point Dunes of Provincetown, Massachusetts, her dog's insistent barking led her to a grim scene—the decaying body of an unidentified woman. Lying eerily close to a nearby road, the remains were surrounded by the buzzing of insects—indicating the time that had passed since the woman's death.

The setting was peculiar, with two distinct sets of footprints leading to where the body lay and tire tracks stopping just 50 yards from the scene. It was speculated that the woman had met her tragic end approximately two weeks before she was found.

The girl, accompanied by her dog, stumbled upon a sight that would forever change the quiet of Cape Cod. The woman's body was severely mutilated; her hands and several teeth were missing—a deliberate act, likely intended to thwart identification and forensic examination. Her life had been violently ended by blunt force trauma, a brutal attack that left no doubt about the malicious intent.

Lying face-down on a beach blanket, the surroundings suggested no sign of struggle. This led investigators to consider that she might have known her killer or perhaps had been caught off guard while asleep. The victim was dressed in a blue bandanna, and a pair of Wrangler jeans was tucked beneath her head, as if to provide a final, unsettling pillow. Her long auburn hair was tied back with a gold-flecked elastic band, and her toenails were painted a bright pink—a stark contrast to the grisly scene.

Initial examinations detailed a woman who stood around 5 feet 6 inches tall, with an athletic build and evidence of costly dental work, estimated between $5,000 and $10,000. Though her exact age was uncertain, it was believed she ranged anywhere from 20 to 49 years old. Her almost decapitated state hinted at strangulation, compounded by a crushing blow to the head, likely delivered with a military-style entrenching tool.

The search for her identity and killer ran cold, and with that, the woman was laid to rest in a quiet October ceremony in 1974. Her burial, marked by a thin metal casket, was intended to bring some semblance of peace, though the case remained stubbornly unsolved. Decades later, in 2014, renewed efforts and compassion from an investigator provided her with a new casket, ensuring her dignity was preserved even as the mystery of her death continued to haunt those dedicated to solving it.

Who was this woman known only as "The Lady of The Dunes"? And why did her life end in such violence? These questions lingered as a chilling echo of a crime shrouded in mystery and desperation.

**Investigation**

The investigation into the mysterious "Lady of the Dunes," was a challenging case that left investigators grasping at straws. Police authorities meticulously sifted through thousands of missing-person files, hoping to link the unidentified victim with someone reported missing. They also examined a list of vehicles permitted to pass through the area, but these efforts regrettably led them to dead ends. No connections were made that could pinpoint her identity.

At the crime scene, an eerie stillness lingered over the dunes. Unnervingly, the sand and the beach blanket remained undisturbed, implying that her lifeless body might have been deliberately placed there. It was as if she had been silently arranged to rest in that exact spot—whether by the hands of her killer or another party remains unknown. Besides the woman's jeans, a bandana, a blanket, and a ponytail holder, no significant evidence surfaced during the extensive searches. The surrounding dunes, with their shifting sands, held their secrets tightly.

In an attempt to bring her story to life, the first facial reconstruction of the woman was crafted from clay in 1979. It was a rudimentary yet hopeful step towards identifying her. Her remains were exhumed in 1980 for further examination, though the findings yielded no new insights. Strangely, her skull was not interred with her body at the time, leaving investigators with an incomplete picture.

Further developments came in March 2000 when her body was unearthed again, this time to extract DNA. Genetic testing brought a glimmer of hope that modern science might reveal her identity or connect her to existing relatives. Despite these efforts, the case continued to baffle authorities. In May 2010, a CT scan of her skull was conducted, generating detailed images that the National Center for Missing and Exploited Children utilized to create a new facial reconstruction. Each step forward in technology seemed to hold new promise, yet the sands of time continued to obscure the truth behind "The Lady of the Dunes."

**Leads**

In 1987, a Canadian woman shared a chilling recollection with a friend. She claimed to have witnessed her father strangling a woman in Massachusetts around 1972. This revelation spurred the local police into action, but despite their efforts, the woman vanished without a trace, leaving investigators with nothing but another frustrating dead end.

Meanwhile, another lead emerged from Boston in 1974, when a woman contacted law enforcement, convinced that the reconstruction of the victim resembled her missing sister. Despite the promising nature of this tip, it, too, failed to yield any concrete results.

The case took another twist with the introduction of Rory Gene Kesinger, a notorious criminal who had escaped from jail in 1973. At 25 years old, she matched the approximate age of the murder victim. Authorities noted a striking resemblance between Kesinger and the Lady of the Dunes, prompting them to follow this lead. However, hope was dashed when DNA testing from Kesinger's mother revealed no match to the victim. Two additional missing women, Francis Ewalt and Vicke Lamberton, were also considered in the investigation, but were ultimately ruled out.

**Jaws film extra possibility**

In August 2015, an unexpected theory reignited interest in the case. Joe Hill, son of famed horror novelist Stephen King, introduced a tantalizing possibility after reading "The Skeleton Crew: How Amateur Sleuths are Solving America's Coldest Cases." Hill proposed that the Lady of the Dunes might have been an extra in the iconic 1975 film "Jaws," which was filmed on Martha's Vineyard. He noticed a woman in the Fourth of July beach scene wearing a blue bandana and jeans, similar to those found with the victim. Although intriguing, this theory was deemed "far-fetched" by some, tempering the initial excitement it generated.

Despite skepticism, Hill's theory breathed new life into the mystery, transforming the Lady of the Dunes into one of the most famous unsolved cases in true crime history. While the connection to "Jaws" remained speculative, it served as a reminder that, even decades later, the enigma of Ruth Marie Terry's murder continued to capture the imagination of amateur sleuths worldwide.

## Identification

In 2022, the breakthrough moment arrived when the skeletal remains of "The Lady of The Dunes" were entrusted to Othram, a state-of-the-art forensic laboratory specializing in DNA analysis. From these bones, silent witnesses to a long-buried mystery, a DNA profile emerged. This genetic blueprint was not just a sequence of nucleotides; it was the key that unlocked a vast network of distant relatives, ultimately leading to the long-awaited identification of the victim.

On October 31, 2022, the Boston FBI field office made a groundbreaking announcement. The woman who had been only known by her grim moniker was finally named as Ruth Marie Terry. For nearly fifty years, this name had been a whisper lost to time, but now it resonated with clarity and certainty.

The path to identifying Terry was anything but straightforward. Investigators had poured their hearts and souls into this case over the decades, employing every available method to give her a name. They canvassed neighborhoods, meticulously combing through thousands of missing-person reports. Artists had crafted clay model facial reconstructions and age-regression sketches, breathing life into the unknown face found in the dunes.

Yet, as the years passed, so too did advancements in technology. New investigative and scientific techniques emerged, offering fresh hope for cases like Ruth Marie Terry's. One such advancement, Investigative Genealogy, became a beacon of possibility. By blending DNA analysis with traditional genealogy research and historical records, this innovative method opened new doors for solving long-cold cases.

The FBI's determination to solve this infamous cold case led them to employ the power of genealogical examination, unraveling the threads of Terry's lineage and providing the definitive confirmation needed to establish her identity. This triumph not only closed a chapter in a decades-old mystery but also showcased the relentless pursuit of justice and the ever-evolving landscape of forensic science.

**Guy Muldavin**

Guy Rockwell Muldavin's story is one of murky motives and mysterious disappearances, weaving a tapestry of intrigue that spans decades. Born on October 27, 1923, in Santa Fe, New Mexico, Muldavin's early life gave no indication of the dark paths he would later traverse.

In 1942, Guy found himself amid the bustling streets of New York City, where he attended the prestigious American Academy of Dramatic Arts. However, his dreams of serving in World War II were dashed due to a mastoid infection, a twist of fate that would see him remain in civilian life.

By 1946, Muldavin had established a seemingly ordinary existence, he married Joellen Mae Loop and eventually working as a professor. The couple's life led them across the country, from New York to California and finally to Seattle, Washington, where Muldavin took up a job as a disk jockey. Yet, their story ended in divorce by 1956.

The shadows began to deepen around Muldavin in 1958 when he married Manzanita Aileen 'Manzy' Ryan in Idaho. Manzanita, who had a daughter named Dolores Ann Mearns, found herself entangled in a chilling mystery. Both Manzy and Dolores vanished on April 1, 1960, leaving behind a trail of questions and suspicions that pointed squarely at Muldavin. His presence became so conspicuous that he fled Seattle, only to be apprehended by the FBI for evading testimony in their disappearance case.

Despite this ominous backdrop, Muldavin's life continued to twist and turn. By July 29, 1960, he married Evelyn Marie Emerson in Washington, and then wed once more in Los Angeles in 1963. His convoluted marital history did not shield him from legal troubles; he faced larceny charges for swindling his third wife's family out of $10,000, coinciding eerily with his second wife's disappearance. Convicted in 1961, his sentence was suspended a year later, contingent on repaying the stolen funds.

True-crime enthusiasts might recognize Muldavin from Ann Rule's 2007 book "Smoke, Mirrors and Murder," which explores the disturbing disappearances of Ryan and Mearns. Investigators discovered dismembered body parts in a septic tank connected to Muldavin, yet frustratingly, the evidence did not definitively link back to the missing women. Lack of concrete proof resulted in no charges being filed, leaving a lingering sense of injustice.

But Muldavin's suspected involvement in sinister activities didn't end there. He remains the prime suspect in the murder of Henry Lawrence "Red" Baird and the mysterious vanishing of Barbara Joe Kelley, a waitress last seen in June 1950. Baird was found dead on the beach near Table Bluff, shot execution-style, with his clothing meticulously arranged, and Barbara was never seen again. These unresolved cases only add layers to the enigma that was Muldavin.

By the late 1970s, Muldavin had relocated to Chualar, California, drawing the attention of local media. Retired from his executive role at a posh silver store in Beverly Hills, he found solace as a volunteer radio host and tobacco shop worker, seemingly leading an innocuous life. But even these later years were overshadowed by his alleged past.

On August 28, 2023, the veil finally lifted—Guy Rockwell Muldavin was officially named as the killer of Ruth Marie Terry, "The Lady of the Dunes." This revelation closed a chapter of unanswered questions while opening a new dialogue about the elusive man at its center. His death in 2002, after a prolonged illness, left lingering questions, but the truth of his life may never be fully uncovered.

**Earlier Suspects**

In the early 1980s, an intriguing lead emerged as investigators closed in on a potential connection between Ruth Marie Terry and the notorious mobster James "Whitey" Bulger. Eyewitness accounts from that era suggested a woman bearing a striking resemblance to Terry had been seen in Bulger's company around the time she met her untimely demise. Known for his ruthless methods, Bulger was infamous for removing the teeth of his victims—a chilling detail that aligned with the grisly state in which Terry's body was discovered. Despite these compelling coincidences, no definitive link has been established between Bulger and the murder. The prospect of justice faded further when Bulger met a violent end himself, murdered in prison in 2018, leaving behind a trail of unanswered questions.

Another suspect who initially drew investigators' attention was Tony Costa, a serial killer who terrorized the Truro area in Massachusetts. Costa, whose reign of terror ended with his death on May 12, 1974, was initially considered a potential perpetrator. However, the timeline of his death and Terry's body being discovered in July of the same year ultimately ruled him out as a suspect. Despite being cleared, Costa's dark legacy lingered as a reminder of the violence that had gripped the region.

**Hadden Clark's Confession**

Enter Hadden Clark, a convicted murderer with a troubled mind who would later entangle himself in the mystery of Ruth Marie Terry's demise. Clark claimed responsibility for the heinous act, weaving a narrative that added another layer to the perplexing case. "I could have told the police what her name was," he allegedly said, "but after they beat the shit out of me, I wasn't going to tell them shit." His cryptic admission was accompanied by a tantalizing detail—that the truth the police sought lay buried in his grandfather's garden.

However, Clark's credibility was undercut by his history of mental illness. Diagnosed with paranoid schizophrenia, Clark's condition often led him to make false confessions, casting doubt on his claims. Despite this, in 2000, Clark led law enforcement to a location where he claimed to have interred two victims two decades earlier. His confession extended beyond Massachusetts, insinuating that he had been responsible for a string of murders across various states from the 1970s to the 1990s.

In 2004, Clark reached out to a friend with a letter that reignited interest in his chilling declarations. He confessed again to a murder on Cape Cod, this time bolstered by two stark illustrations—a haunting sketch of a handless, naked woman lying face down, and a map detailing the location where Terry's body was discovered. Whether his confession was the product of a disturbed mind or a glimpse of the truth remains a puzzle. His claims, steeped in mystery and uncertainty, continue to be a dark shadow over the Lady of the Dunes case.

The saga of the "Lady of the Dunes," which has haunted the collective consciousness for decades, is a poignant reminder of the complexities that shroud many true crime cases. The mysterious death of Ruth Marie Terry and the gnawing questions of her identity encapsulated a narrative filled with half-truths, dead ends, and chilling. Despite these uncertainties, the identification of Guy Rockwell Muldavin as her killer posthumously brings a bittersweet closure to the story. Although Muldavin lived the remainder of his life free from the justice he eluded, the revelation of his guilt provides some solace in the pursuit of truth, granting Ruth Marie Terry her long-deserved identity—a rare resolution in the world of unsolved crimes.

# CHAPTER TEN

## A MURDER IN ROOM 636 – THE TALE OF ALBERT KNOX

San Antonio, a city renowned for its vibrant culture and historic landmarks, also holds the somber title of being one of the most haunted cities in America. Among its many tales of the supernatural, the Sheraton-Gunter Hotel stands out, not just for its storied past but for the chilling events that unfolded within its walls. Whether you're a skeptic or a believer in the paranormal, the haunting tale linked to this historic establishment is bound to capture your imagination and send shivers down your spine.

When people conjure images of San Antonio's rich history, the Alamo inevitably springs to mind. Its tales of bravery and sacrifice are woven into the very fabric of Texas lore. Yet, beyond these iconic stories lies the Sheraton-Gunter Hotel—a silent witness to the city's tumultuous past. This hotel, nestled in the heart of San Antonio, has borne witness to both the triumphs and tragedies that have shaped the city, including a particularly gruesome chapter that refuses to fade into obscurity.

## History

The land beneath the Sheraton-Gunter Hotel has been home to a hotel since 1837, just a year following the legendary Battle of the Alamo. Over the decades, it has transformed and evolved, yet its essence as a place of gathering and refuge has remained constant. From 1846 to 1847, it was known as the Vance House hotel, serving as a strategic administrative base during the Mexican-American War. The echoes of military strategy and the clash of nations reverberated through its halls, setting the stage for the stories yet to come.

During the Civil War, the location witnessed a significant moment in history when Confederate forces, in a daring move, secured $1.6 million in federal property—a victory that underscored the ongoing struggle and turmoil of the era. The narrative of the Gunter Hotel truly began in 1909 when it was constructed into an impressive eight-story building boasting over 300 rooms. Throughout the years, ownership of the hotel changed hands numerous times, each transition adding new layers to its rich tapestry until it ultimately became the Sheraton-Gunter Hotel in 1999.

However, beneath the charm and elegance of this historic establishment lies the dark story of a murder that forever stained its legacy. In 1965, Room 636 became the scene of a chilling crime involving Albert Knox, a man whose actions echoed through time, leaving a permanent scar on the hotel's reputation. The details of this event are as mysterious as they are disturbing, challenging those who hear the story to ponder the thin line between the past and present, reality and the spectral unknown.

The tale of the Sheraton-Gunter Hotel serves as a compelling reminder of the shadows that dwell in even the most inviting places. Prepare to be drawn into a world where history and the paranormal intertwine, creating a narrative that will leave you questioning the very nature of the spirits that linger in San Antonio's haunted heart.

**February 6, 1965 – A Day Like Any Other, Or Was It?**

February 6, 1965, started off like any other day at the Gunter Hotel. Guests bustled in and out, staff attended to their duties, and the sun cast a warm glow over the historic building. Yet, unbeknownst to anyone, something sinister was about to unfold within its walls.

Among the influx of guests, a man with striking blonde hair, appearing to be in his late 30s, caught the attention of the reception desk. He introduced himself as "Albert Knox" and was handed the key to room 636. On the surface, he was just another hotel guest. But for those who took notice, there was something slightly off about him

Over the following days, Knox became a familiar figure, frequently seen making his way through the hotel lobby. By his side was an intriguing blonde woman of a similar age. Her presence turned heads, and whispers circulated among the staff and guests alike. Some speculated she was a call girl; others merely observed the mysterious allure that surrounded her.

The pair exuded an air of intrigue and secrecy, their comings and goings shrouded in a veil of speculation.

Were they mere acquaintances caught up in the whirlwind of a sultry affair, or was there a deeper story hidden beneath their polished exteriors?

Eyewitnesses recalled seeing Knox with a drink in hand more often than not. Rumors spread quickly—some claimed he was attempting to recover from a particularly wild drinking spree, while others insisted he was still reveling in his vices, with no intention of slowing down anytime soon.

One thing was certain, though. The spectacle of their lavish, carefree lifestyle was equal parts mesmerizing and alarming. Knox seemed content to immerse himself in a world of chaos and indulgence, a reprieve from reality, perhaps before retreating to the safety and familiarity of his parents' home.

Yet, amid the clinking of glasses and laughter echoing through the hotel corridors, darkness lingered—a premonition of the twist that fate was about to deliver. Just what secrets did room 636 hold, and what truth lay buried beneath the guise of "Albert Knox"?

For those at the Gunter Hotel, it would soon become clear that this was no ordinary guest, and his story was far from over.

### A Chilling Discovery at The Gunter

The quiet ambiance of The Gunter Hotel was shattered on the morning of February 8th, painting an entirely new image of the once-peaceful establishment. Maria Luisa Guerra, a diligent maid finishing her shift that afternoon, approached the notorious room 636. The "Do Not Disturb" sign hung ominously on the door, an all-too-common oversight by departing guests. Assuming it was nothing out of the ordinary, Maria pushed the door open, completely unaware of the horrors awaiting her on the other side.

Inside, the scene that unfolded was more nightmarish than any of Maria's darkest imaginings. Standing amidst the chaos was a tall Anglo man, seemingly composed despite the heinous tableau around him. The bed was drenched with blood, its sheets resembling a macabre canvas of violence that spoke volumes without uttering a single word. The room was a chaotic symphony of crimson, its walls bearing witness to the unspeakable acts committed in their presence.

Maria's instinctive scream pierced the eerie silence, a primal reaction to the ghastly spectacle before her. The man, later identified as Albert Knox, responded not with panic, but with an eerie calmness. He placed a finger to his lips, and gave Maria a "Shhhh," a command for quiet that seemed almost surreal given the gravity of the situation. With unnerving composure, he gathered up the bundle of blood-soaked sheets and calmly exited the room, leaving Maria rooted in shock.

Despite Maria's swift report to hotel management, it took a nerve-wracking forty minutes before action was taken. By then, Knox had vanished, leaving behind a room that was now a crime scene demanding immediate attention.

When the police arrived, they were greeted by a chilling array of evidence. Empty wine bottles, scattered olives and cheese, and the foreboding presence of small, bloody footprints painted a vivid picture of the night's events. Strands of blonde hair, nylon hose, and women's underclothing were discovered, each piece a clue in the unfolding mystery.

A fired .22 caliber shell lay abandoned on the bed, its corresponding slug embedded in the wall near a chair smeared with blood. The detectives noted a grisly pattern of blood trails leading back and forth to the bathroom, suggesting the killer's repeated visits for reasons unknown at the time. Detective Walter "Corky" Dennis reflected on the scene, remarking, "It was the bloodiest place I had ever seen up until then. The bathroom was especially bad and just sticky with blood all over the place. We noticed the bathtub had a red ring around it like it had been drained of blood." This gruesome detail hinted at the horrific possibility that the murderer had dismembered and washed the victim's body in the tub before discreetly removing it.

In the days leading up to the chilling events at The Gunter Hotel, a mysterious figure skulking about San Antonio captured the curiosity of many. Known only as Albert Knox, he was seen at the bustling Sears Department Store on Romaine Plaza, his presence both unassuming and perplexing. On that day, Knox's frustration simmered when he was told that the store lacked the large meat grinder he desperately sought. The store clerk, eager to assist, suggested ordering from the warehouse—an idea Knox dismissed with visible irritation before storming out. His impatience that day now seems a sinister precursor to the events that would soon unfold.

The murder in Room 636 remains shrouded in mystery and speculation. Forensic experts remain divided on whether the room served as the gruesome site of a butchering. Some experts point to the significant blood evidence, supporting the theory of a gruesome act. Others argue the opposite, claiming the scene did not bear enough blood traces for such an event. This uncertainty continues to haunt investigators and historians.

The investigation took a shocking turn when law enforcement uncovered that "Albert Knox" was an alias for Walter Emerick, a 37-year-old accountant who had fallen on hard times. With this revelation, a statewide alert was issued. Hours later, a new lead emerged—a security guard at the St. Anthony Hotel, just a stone's throw from The Gunter, reported a tenant going by "Robert Ashley" who aroused suspicion by refusing maid service.

Police quickly mobilized to room 536, where Ashley resided. The plan was to catch him unaware, but nerves got the better of the security guard assisting them. The keys rattled conspicuously as they approached the door, alerting the occupant. Before the detectives could enter, a gunshot echoed through the hotel corridor. Detective Frank Castillion recounted the grim scene that followed—they found the suspect, Walter Emerick, lifeless from a self-inflicted gunshot wound to the temple.

Inside the room, police discovered incriminating evidence linking Emerick to the crime at The Gunter. Fingerprints matched those found in the infamous Room 636, and a bloodstained white shirt, painstakingly scrubbed clean, hinted at a desperate attempt to erase traces of his crimes.

Yet, the case remains unsolved. The body of the mysterious blonde woman, believed to be connected to the events of that night, has never been found. No missing person's report fits her description, leaving a haunting void in the narrative.

The Gunter Hotel carries an eerie legacy. Staff and guests have long reported strange occurrences—a spectral presence in the hallways leading to the former Room 636. Jackie Contreras, a former staff member, vividly recalls the day she encountered what she believes to be a ghost. In 1990, preparing the room for important clients, she opened the door to find it shrouded in darkness. The typical sunlight that streamed through the windows was absent. Reaching for the light switch, the dim glow from the hallway revealed a woman standing eerily still, arms outstretched. Pale and aged, she looked directly at Contreras, who fled in terror. Front desk staff assured her that no one was staying in the room.

Further unsettling evidence came that same year during the hotel's Christmas party. Staff photos revealed a recurring, inexplicable figure—a ghostly presence captured over and over again, lurking in the background.

In a bid to quell the supernatural activity, Room 636 was divided into two separate rooms, yet the intrigue remains. Guests are invited to experience these haunted quarters, feeling the chill of its storied past.

For those daring enough to explore, The Gunter Hotel awaits your stay. Will you spend a night where history and mystery intertwine?

# CHAPTER ELEVEN

## THE CIRCLEVILLE LETTERS

In the quiet corridors of Circleville, Ohio, an eerie mystery began to unfold in the late 1970s—a mystery that would bewilder and capture the imagination of the town's residents. This was a story not just about letters, but about secrets whispered in shadows, veiled threats, and a riddle that remains unsolved to this day.

**A Town Bewildered by Anonymous Threats**

The tranquility of Circleville, a small, tight-knit community nestled just a short drive from Columbus, was shattered in 1977. It all began with a seemingly innocuous piece of mail delivered to Mary Gillispie, a local school bus driver. This letter, however, was anything but ordinary. In stark, menacing words, the anonymous writer declared, "I've been watching your house, and I know you have children." The demand that followed was cryptic yet loaded with danger—"Stay away from Massie."

For Mary, the message was painfully clear. Someone had unearthed her secret affair with Gordon Massie, the school superintendent. What should have been a private matter was now at the mercy of an unseen tormentor. But Mary's plight was not unique. Across Circleville, from modest homes to bustling businesses and even government offices, hundreds of similar letters began to appear. No one was safe from the pervasive reach of the mysterious writer.

### The Sinister Intent Behind the Letters

In the quaint town of Circleville, the letters came without warning—harbingers of fear crafted with a deliberate hand. These were not mere scribbles; they were calculated strategies of intimidation, each one insidiously revealing personal details that only a vigilant observer could possess. What drove the anonymous author to pen such letters? Was it sheer malice, a perverse sense of justice, or an agenda far darker than anyone dared to imagine?

Residents found themselves plunged into a whirlpool of paranoia, their once harmonious community now engulfed by suspicion. Neighbors exchanged wary glances, each wondering if the person who lived next door could be the malevolent mind behind the letters. The seemingly serene facade of Circleville threatened to crack under the weight of hidden truths, long buried but now dangerously close to emerging in a wave of scandal. Despite the palpable tension, the identity of the mysterious scribe remained a tantalizing enigma, evading all attempts to unmask them.

The impact of the Circleville letters went beyond sowing seeds of chaos; they broke apart families and ruptured friendships, casting a dark shadow over the town. Accusations flew, and trust was fractured, leaving residents questioning why their peaceful town had been chosen as the target of such venomous scrutiny. How could someone know so much about them, and why would they wield this knowledge as a weapon?

Extensive investigations ensued, each promising a breakthrough yet delivering none. The author of the letters remained veiled in mystery, leaving behind a legacy of unanswered questions. Eventually, the letters ceased, but not before leaving deep scars on the collective memory of the community.

**The Mysterious Death of Ron Gillispie**

The unsettling wave of anonymous letters shattered the peace. At the eye of this storm was Mary Gillispie. But soon, the venomous correspondence took a more sinister turn, targeting her husband, Ron Gillispie.

The letters Ron received were not just accusatory; they were menacing. One starkly warned, "Mr. Gillispie, your wife is seeing Gordon Massie." It urged him to adopt violent measures against those involved. For Ron, a man deeply embedded in the fabric of Circleville, the letters were a chilling departure from the norm. They suggested a web of deceit and treachery that seemed out of place in the town's serene backdrop.

Unyielding to the growing threats that loomed large over his family, Ron took matters into his own hands. On an August evening in 1977, after receiving a cryptic phone call, his demeanor changed dramatically—agitation replaced his usual calm. Before leaving, he grabbed his .22

caliber revolver and told his daughter of his intent to confront the mysterious letter writer. Yet, this confrontation would never come to pass.

Later that evening, Ron's truck was discovered crashed against a tree in an unspectacular corner of Circleville. The police deemed it an accident. However, the locals whispered of darker forces at play. Paul Freshour, Ron's brother-in-law, was particularly adamant in his disbelief of the accident narrative. For him, Ron's death reeked of something more insidious. Adding to the mystery was the discovery that Ron's gun had fired once before the crash, a confounding detail that hinted at a deadly encounter.

These events left an indelible mark on Circleville, transforming it from a haven of rural charm into the setting of an unsolved mystery. The specter of the anonymous letters and the untimely demise of a beloved local figure fueled a mystery that would be dissected for years. The questions lingered long after the dust settled—who was the puppeteer behind the letters, and what role did they play in the tragic fate of Ron Gillispie?

Even after Ron Gillispie's tragic death, the sinister barrage of threatening letters flooding the small town of Circleville showed no signs of stopping. Mary Gillispie, his widow, remained ensnared in the web of this anonymous tormentor. The letters taunted her with accusations and veiled threats, one chillingly stating, "Everyone knows what you have done." In a turn of events in 1983, the danger these letters represented took a terrifyingly tangible form. While conducting her usual school bus route, Mary was confronted with a sign targeting her teenage daughter. As she attempted to dismantle this offensive display, she stumbled upon a trap—a box rigged with a loaded gun, set to go off upon tampering. Her swift reflexes saved her from what could have been a deadly encounter.

This narrowly averted tragedy provided law enforcement with a crucial investigative thread to follow. Upon tracing the gun's serial number, investigators connected it to Paul Freshour, Ron's brother-in-law, an individual currently embroiled in a bitter divorce. His estranged wife, Karen Sue, further implicated him by alleging that she had discovered the malicious letters concealed within their home. Despite Freshour's vehement denials, a failed polygraph test branded him a liar, and the evidence led to his arrest. In 1984, Freshour faced trial and was convicted for attempted murder, seemingly bringing an end to the dark saga that had haunted Circleville. Yet, questions lingered about the true orchestrator behind the letters and whether justice had indeed been served.

**Doubts and New Suspicions**

Despite finding himself behind bars, Paul Freshour claimed his innocence, and intriguingly, the letters continued to flow. This persistence puzzled many, especially given that the prison warden himself verified that Freshour did not have access to writing materials. These facts cast doubt on the prosecution's narrative, prompting fresh inquiries into the true identity of the enigmatic Circleville writer.

At trial, Freshour's defense team posed a compelling question: who would bear such intense animosity towards him to orchestrate the letters' campaign? The finger was pointed toward Karen Sue and her boyfriend, with the latter's description suspiciously aligning with eyewitness accounts of someone seen setting up one of the ominous traps. The speculation added layers to an already complex case, leaving more questions than answers.

The mystery gained national attention in 1993 when the television program "Unsolved Mysteries" took up the case. Adding another twist to the tale, the show itself received a chilling letter from the anonymous writer, further complicating the narrative. Then, as if following the script of a suspense thriller, the saga of the Circleville letters abruptly came to a close. Coincidentally, this happened the same year Freshour was granted parole in 1994. With his release, the letters ceased entirely, leaving the true author hidden in the shadows, and the town of Circleville forever haunted by unanswered questions.

### An Unresolved Mystery

The Circleville letters have captivated many, standing as a mysterious and unsettling chapter in the town's history. Despite various attempts to unearth the truth over the years, these letters have evaded resolution. While countless theories circulate, none have provided the conclusive answers that both locals and investigators yearn for. The mystery retains its grip, seemingly impervious to the passage of time and the scrutiny of keen minds.

Recent forensic advancements have shed some light on this mystery, suggesting a possible connection between the handwriting of Paul Freshour and the letters. However, the evidence remains inconclusive, leaving even the most meticulous sleuths stumped. This uncertainty feeds into the broader allure for true crime aficionados, who find themselves drawn into a web of suspense and intrigue.

For the residents of Circleville, and indeed for all who relish a good mystery, the tale of these anonymous letters serves as a haunting reminder of vengeance cloaked in secrecy. It stands as a testament to the enduring power of anonymity and the stubborn persistence of secrets that refuse to emerge from the shadows, no matter how fervently they are pursued.

# CHAPTER TWELVE

## THE YUBA COUNTY FIVE

In the late winter of 1978, the quiet community of Yuba County was shaken by the disappearance of five young men, each navigating life with mild intellectual challenges or psychiatric conditions. This group, affectionately known as "the boys," included Ted Weiher, Jack Huett, Bill Sterling, Jack Madruga, and Gary Mathias. They vanished after attending a college basketball game at California State University, Chico, on February 24th—a night meant to be filled with camaraderie and sportsmanship.

These men were not just friends; they were teammates on the Gateway Gators, a basketball team sponsored by a local vocational training center. The following day, they were scheduled to participate in their own game in Rocklin, near Sacramento. But as the clock ticked past 10 PM on February 24th, the Yuba County Five were never seen alive again.

Their disappearance has since become a haunting mystery, one that echoes through the dense expanses of the Plumas

National Forest. For nearly five decades, this case has both baffled and intrigued people worldwide, earning its place as America's version of the Dyatlov Pass incident, although with far more authentic and potentially sinister undertones.

Days after the boys were reported missing, Jack Madruga's 1969 Mercury Montego was discovered abandoned on a desolate mountain dirt road deep in the forest. The vehicle was in perfect working condition and could have easily been freed from the snowdrift it was trapped in, further deepening the enigma. Why had they deviated so far from their route back to Yuba County?

The mystery intensified when the snow thawed in June. Ted Weiher's body was found in a U.S. Forest Service trailer, some twelve miles north of the Mercury's last known location. His tragic end hinted at a prolonged struggle for survival—he had succumbed to starvation despite an abundance of food and supplies nearby. Strangely, his shoes were missing, replaced by those of Gary Mathias, suggesting that Mathias, whose whereabouts remain unknown, was also present in the trailer for some time.

The remains of Jack Madruga, Bill Sterling, and Jackie Huett were discovered scattered in the vicinity, reduced to bones by the ravages of wildlife. The chilling circumstances prompted questions about what happened during those last, desperate weeks in the wilderness.

A witness later emerged, claiming he had spent that same eerie night within earshot of the boys' abandoned car. He recounted hearing voices and seeing flashlight beams, yet his cries for assistance were met with a haunting silence.

These perplexing clues lend credence to theories of foul play, casting a shadow over what might have driven the Yuba County Five into the wilderness. The investigation remains open, an unsolved case that continues to captivate true crime enthusiasts and mystery lovers alike. The story of the Yuba County Five is a puzzle with pieces that refuse to fit, a testament to the strange and unyielding mysteries that lurk just beyond the edge of our understanding.

---

Gary Mathias, a young man with a turbulent past, found himself returning home to the small community of Marysville in Yuba County in the early 1970s after serving in the United States Army in West Germany. During his time overseas, Mathias succumbed to the pitfalls of substance abuse, eventually leading to a diagnosis of schizophrenia. This diagnosis brought an end to his military career and saw him discharged on psychiatric grounds.

Back in Marysville, Mathias began treatment at a local mental health facility. The path to stability was fraught with challenges, marked by moments of aggression and hospitalizations at the local Veterans Administration hospital. Yet, by 1978, Mathias had transitioned to outpatient treatment, taking medications like Stelazine and Cogentin. His physicians considered him a beacon of success, a testament to effective psychiatric care.

Mathias's life extended beyond his medical struggles. He worked with his stepfather's gardening business, supplementing his Army disability pay, and had formed a close-knit friendship with four other young men from nearby Yuba City and Marysville. This group, affectionately dubbed "the boys" by their families, shared a deep bond rooted in mutual understanding and camaraderie. Two of them, Ted Weiher and Jackie Huett, navigated life with intellectual disabilities, while Jack Madruga and Bill Sterling were often seen as "slow learners." Despite these labels, each man brought a unique spark to the group.

Ted Weiher was lovingly recalled by his brothers, Dallas and Perry, as a "gentle giant," while Madruga, who hailed from Yuba City, was known for his intelligence and quiet demeanor. Sterling, an avid bowler, was celebrated for his sweetness, while Mathias's musical talent and athleticism were fondly remembered by those who knew him. Jackie Huett, the youngest at 24, was cherished for his kindness and loyalty—a true friend to all.

The boys first crossed paths through a basketball team organized by a Yuba County nonprofit dedicated to supporting individuals with disabilities. Their passion for sports was infectious, and they spent countless hours playing and watching games together. One of their shared interests was following the UC Davis basketball team.

On February 24, 1978, this shared love for basketball lured them to Chico, where UC Davis was set to face off against Chico State. Piling into Madruga's car, the five set out eagerly, familiar with the route from previous visits. An editor from the Chico newspaper later recalled spotting the group at the game, drawn to their distinct presence.

These gatherings, whether to play or watch sports, were the boys' sanctuary—a place where they could be themselves without judgment. Known as the Gateway Gators, their basketball team thrived under the auspices of a local program supporting individuals with mental disabilities.

While their lives were not without challenge, the Yuba County Five found solace, joy, and unity in each other's company, bonded by the simple pleasures of friendship and sport.

**Vanishing into the Night**

On February 25, a sense of excitement filled the air for the five young men from Yuba County, California. They were eagerly preparing for a weeklong basketball tournament sponsored by the Special Olympics, with a tantalizing reward awaiting the victors—a free trip to Los Angeles.

The night before the big game, the group meticulously laid out their uniforms, each detail carefully attended to. Some even asked their parents to wake them up early, ensuring they wouldn't miss a moment of the action. That evening, however, a spontaneous decision saw them heading north to Chico, to cheer on the UC Davis basketball team against Chico State. Jack Madruga, one of the two licensed drivers among them, took the wheel of his turquoise and white 1969 Mercury Montego, leading them on a 50-mile venture.

The crisp air of a February night in the Sacramento Valley enveloped them, yet they wore only light coats, seemingly unfazed by the chill. After witnessing UC Davis' victory, the quintet visited Behr's Market in downtown Chico, grabbing refreshments—snacks, sodas, and milk—just before the store's closing time. The clerk, somewhat irked by their late arrival, remembered them distinctly.

That fleeting encounter became the last confirmed sighting of the Yuba County Five. At home, their families waited expectantly for a joyous return that never came. When morning dawned without their arrival, concern turned to action, and the police were alerted.

The sudden disappearance sent shockwaves through their tight-knit community, where everyone knew one another. "They were different boys," noted Perry, reflecting on the unique nature of each young man. Their absence was deeply felt, creating an unsettling atmosphere in a town where such mysteries were unheard of.

The stakes were high for the five friends; Disneyland tickets were on the line at the tournament. For these men, missing the game was unthinkable. "They were going to get home come hell or high water," insisted Wright, highlighting just how determined they were.

Four days later, a chilling discovery was made—Madruga's car, found abandoned in snow on the Oroville Quincy Highway in Butte County, over 70 miles off course. The vehicle, eerily intact and undamaged, lay waiting, windows down as if inviting the harsh winter air. Inside, remnants of their Chico pit stop—candy wrappers and milk cartons—were scattered about, along with maps that spoke to Madruga's fondness for navigation.

Brian Bernardis, the cold case investigator for the Yuba County Sheriff's Office, has given many interviews over the years on this case. Reflecting on the scene, he observed, "There was nothing to indicate foul play or any sinister activity." Yet, the car's presence in such an unlikely location posed more questions than answers, deepening the enigma.

Initially, the local authorities in Butte and Yuba counties focused their search efforts along the route the men had taken to Chico. Despite their diligent efforts, there was no trace of the group or their vehicle.

A breakthrough came days later, when a ranger from Plumas National Forest recalled an encounter that would eventually become a crucial lead. He had come across a Montego Mercury, abandoned along Oroville-Quincy Road on February 25. At the time, the sight wasn't particularly alarming; the area was frequented by residents heading into the Sierra Nevadas for winter activities like cross-country skiing.

It wasn't until the ranger stumbled upon a missing persons bulletin that he realized the significance of the vehicle he had seen. Acting on this revelation, he quickly informed the investigators, guiding them to the location of the car on February 28. This discovery marked the beginning of an investigation that would capture the attention of the nation.

## Sightings

What became of them was a question that haunted the region, sparking media frenzy and a flood of speculative reports.

Amidst the sea of sightings and hearsay, two reports emerged, standing out like beacons in the murky waters of uncertainty. The first came from Joseph Schons, a Sacramento resident whose tale was as compelling as it was eerie. On the night of February 24th, Schons found himself on a routine mission to check the snowpack near his cabin, preparing for a family ski adventure. But fate had other plans. His car, like many caught in the clutch of winter, became ensnared in the drifts of snow.

While wrestling with the predicament, Schons felt the onset of what he later realized was a heart attack. Stricken and alone in the cold, he crawled back into his car to wait out the night. It was then, through a haze of pain and fear, that he noticed the unusual activity. Headlights pierced the darkness, illuminating a scene that defied explanation. A car parked behind his own, surrounded by figures—one of whom Schons imagined as a woman cradling a baby. His calls for help were met with silence, the figures extinguishing their lights at his cries.

What haunted Schons more than the night itself was what he recalled next—flickering flashlights and the whisper of voices beyond his reach. Did he truly witness a pickup truck pull up and drive away, or was it the fevered imaginings of a tormented mind? By dawn, as his pain ebbed slightly, Schons mustered the strength to trek down to a nearby lodge, his path crossing that of the abandoned Mercury Montego—the very car linked to the missing men.

In parallel, an equally intriguing account surfaced from a store owner in the small town of Brownsville, approximately 30 miles from where the Montego was found. Her claim added a puzzling twist. On March 3rd, she reported, four of the young men visited her store in a red pickup truck, just a day after their disappearance. They seemed out of place—she noted their wide eyes and unfamiliar expressions. Two remained outside in a phone booth, while the others ventured in to buy supplies. Her account was bolstered by the store owner's testimony, which painted a picture of odd yet telling behavior.

The unusual nature of their interaction struck a chord with those who knew the group, particularly when brothers of the missing men remarked on the oddity of such a trip during a basketball game. Yet, descriptions of their behavior—the peculiar choice of food and the aversion to telephones—hinted at potential truths buried within the narrative.

The unfolding enigma of the Yuba County Five gripped the hearts of many, fueling a relentless search for answers. Was Schons' vision of figures on the mountain a mirage, or a glimpse into a darker reality? Did the men indeed make a stop at the Brownsville store, only to vanish once more into the ether? The questions lingered, casting a long shadow that true crime enthusiasts and mystery lovers would ponder for years to come.

### The Unsettling Discovery

A perplexing discovery was made of a car abandoned deep in the Plumas National Forest. This car, belonging to Jack Madruga, was found 70 miles from Chico, far from any direct route to the men's intended destination in Yuba City or Marysville. Inside, remnants of their day were haphazardly left behind—empty wrappers and programs from a basketball game, accompanied by a neatly folded map of California. Yet, why had these men ventured so deep into the wilderness without any apparent reason, especially on a frigid winter night?

Jack Madruga's family was bewildered; Jack detested the cold and was unfamiliar with mountain roads. Why, then, was his car stranded at 4,400 feet amidst snowdrifts, just shy of where the road closed for winter? The car itself bore no signs of distress—no dents or mud scrapes marred its pristine undercarriage. The engine roared to life with ease when hot-wired by the police, and the gas tank still held a quarter full. All five men, young and fit, could have easily pushed the car free of the light snow that trapped it. Yet, the car was abandoned with a window rolled down, an act entirely out of character for the cautious Madruga.

Efforts to locate the men were thwarted by a harsh snowstorm, turning the rescue operation into a perilous endeavor. Even snowcat searchers found themselves lost in the unforgiving labyrinth of the forest. The search was temporarily suspended due to relentless weather, leaving only the abandoned car as a stoic testament to their mysterious disappearance.

Months passed, and despair turned to grim discovery when motorcyclists stumbled upon a body in a remote cabin used by fire crews. The smell of decay lingered in the air as they found Ted Weiher, lifeless and wrapped in blankets, a tragic symbol of a desperate struggle against the elements. His body bore the grim signs of starvation, despite an abundance of food stored nearby. Oddly, Gary Mathias's shoes lay inside while Ted's boots were nowhere to be found, suggesting an unsettling exchange between the two.

The fate of Weiher stood out as particularly perplexing. The trailer, nestled in the remote wilderness, seemed untouched by the life-saving measures one might have expected. No fire flickered in the fireplace, despite the abundance of matches and paperback novels that could have easily served as kindling. It was as if an invisible hand had prevented him from taking the steps that might have ensured his survival.

Adding to this mystery was the fact that the trailer contained heavy forestry clothing, garments capable of providing warmth against the biting cold. Yet, these remained untouched, cloistered away in their place as if awaiting an owner who never returned. Investigators found evidence of sustenance in the form of a dozen opened C-ration cans, their contents consumed, hinting at a desperate attempt to stave off hunger. But mere feet away lay an unopened locker brimming with dehydrated foods—enough provisions to nourish all five men for a year. It seemed implausible that such a resource had gone unnoticed by Weiher or his companions.

Outside the trailer, another mystery awaited. Nearby, a shed housed a butane tank with a valve that, if opened, would have powered the trailer's heating system, warding off the lethal cold. Yet, like the food locker, it too remained untouched, perpetually dormant.

For those who dared to unravel the truth, the case of Weiher was a riddle wrapped in a mystery, a tale of survival that defied logic and reason. What unseen forces, what unspoken fears, kept the necessary steps for survival just out of reach?

The tragedy deepened with the discovery of Bill Sterling and Jack Madruga's bodies on a road miles away, and Jackie Huett's remains a mere mile from Ted's resting place. The heart-wrenching discovery of Jackie's remains by his own father added another layer of sorrow. Four members of the group lay dead, seemingly lost to the wilderness, while Gary Mathias vanished completely, leaving only questions in his wake.

Theories abounded—was the group coerced into the mountains? A promise of adventure or a cruel trick? Rumors swirled of altercations at a convenience store, whispers of a town bully's confessions, yet none led to conclusive answers. Gary Mathias, with his troubled past and mysterious disappearance, emerged as a person of interest—did he hold the key to unraveling this enigma, or was he too a victim of the forest's insidious grip?

**Theories About Their Fate**

Even with the discovery of four of the five men's bodies nestled in the unforgiving terrain of the Sierra Nevadas, investigators were left puzzling over the mysterious circumstances leading to their tragic demise. What compelled these men to venture into such a remote area? Definitive answers remained elusive.

The police speculated that Gary Mathias might have suggested a detour to visit friends in the quaint town of Forbestown. This unexpected excursion could have taken a disastrous turn when the men mistakenly veered off course near Oroville, unwittingly setting them on the treacherous mountain road that would become a path to tragedy.

Why they abandoned their trusty Montego remains unclear. Rather than retracing their steps towards safety—past the lodge that Joseph Schons would later find in more dire circumstances—they pressed onward, down the snow-laden road, driven by some unseen force or perhaps sheer determination.

Curiously, just a day before their disappearance, a U.S. Forest Service snowcat had ventured into the area, clearing snow from a trailer roof to prevent collapse. This activity left behind tracks, which the group might have followed, hoping that shelter lay just beyond the towering 4-6 foot snowdrifts. Sadly, it is believed that Ted Madruga and Jack Sterling succumbed to hypothermia midway through this arduous trek, with Jackie Huett meeting a similar fate soon after.

Upon discovering the trailer, which could have provided much-needed refuge, the surviving men smashed a window to gain entry. Their reluctance to use the supplies inside suggests they feared repercussions, possibly believing they were trespassing on private property.

When John Weiher passed away, or perhaps when Mathias perceived him as deceased, desperation might have driven Mathias to seek civilization, attempting to escape the clutches of the merciless wilderness. Yet, his fate remains a mystery.

## An Unsolved Mystery

The tale of the Yuba County Five remains one of the most perplexing mysteries in true crime history. It's a case riddled with unanswered questions and chilling uncertainties, capturing the imagination of true crime enthusiasts and mystery lovers. What drove these five young men to make a fatal detour into the treacherous wilderness of the

Plumas National Forest? Why did they abandon the safety of their vehicle to traverse an unfamiliar and perilous path on foot?

Speculation has been rife, with the most plausible theory suggesting that Matthias, one of the group members, had friends in the nearby town of Forbestown. Perhaps, in their drive from Chico, the men intended to visit these friends but mistakenly took an ominous wrong turn at Oroville. The road diverged—one leading safely toward Forbestown, the other a desolate path where their car was eventually discovered, abandoned.

Yet, cracks appear in this hypothesis. The group was last seen around 10 PM, making an impromptu visit unlikely given the late hour and the anticipation of a basketball game the following day. Furthermore, if Matthias truly knew the way to Forbestown, would he not have recognized the error before leading his friends deeper into the unknown?

Even more puzzling is why none of the men used the supplies readily available in the trailer they eventually reached. Weiher, described by his parents as somewhat lacking in common sense, might have hesitated to help himself to food that wasn't his. But surely Matthias, a former military man with survival training, would not have allowed their situation to become so dire. The presence of opened cans suggests Matthias was indeed there, but why did survival instincts not kick in sooner to save them all?

None of the offered theories satisfyingly explain every aspect of the tragedy. Perhaps an urgent medical emergency forced their hand—a sudden illness or injury prompting a hurried escape from their vehicle in search of help. Plummeting temperatures and inadequate clothing would have quickly compounded their plight, making survival a tenuous prospect at best.

Despite the exhaustive investigations, the mystery only deepens. With limited remains recovered and crucial details lost to time, the truth remains agonizingly out of reach. The eerie absence of a definitive narrative only adds to the haunting allure of the Yuba County Five case.

Bernardis, reflecting on the baffling events, encapsulates the persistent enigma succinctly, "We know nothing. From that point, we know nothing. They literally disappeared into nowhere."

The disappearance of these five men stands as a sobering reminder of how the mundane can swiftly spiral into the extraordinary, leaving behind more questions than answers. What truly happened on that routine drive through Yuba County? It's a mystery that, for now, remains unresolved, echoing through the corridors of true crime history—a poignant testament to the unpredictability of human fate.

# CHAPTER THIRTEEN

## THE MONSTER OF FLORENCE

In the tangled tapestry of Italy's rich history, one chilling narrative stands out—a story of terror and intrigue that has baffled investigators for decades. The Monster of Florence, known locally as Il Mostro di Firenze, is the enigmatic figure behind a series of gruesome murders that haunted the serene landscapes of Florence from 1968 to 1985. This serial killer's legacy is marked by the brutal slaying of 16 victims, predominantly young couples seeking solitude amidst the whispering woods under the cover of new moons.

Despite an army of criminologists, psychologists, and sociologists from around the globe lending their expertise to solve this grim puzzle, the case stubbornly remains unsolved. Over the years, it has become one of the most perplexing mysteries of criminology, a cold case swirling with shadows of doubt and unanswered questions.

The Italian authorities made significant strides in 2000 when two men were convicted for their roles in four of the double homicides attributed to the Monster. The courtroom drama was heightened by bizarre revelations as the press dubbed the accused duo "Snack Buddies"—a name derived from the odd defense claim that they were merely friends who indulged in casual dining escapades at local eateries. It was a comically absurd twist in a narrative steeped in horror.

Evidence pointed to a chilling modus operandi; multiple weapons were wielded by the killer, including a .22 caliber Beretta handgun and a knife. The brutality of the acts was underscored by the grim mutilation of the female victims, with sections of skin around the sex organs meticulously excised—a signature that added a sinister layer to the killer's identity.

While trials have come and gone and suspects have been imprisoned, the true mastermind—the Monster—remains at large in the realm of speculation and fear. The case continues to captivate those who dare to look into the abyss, a haunting reminder of the darkness that can lurk behind history's more picturesque facades.

---

The Florentine landscape, shrouded by the cover of night, became a hunting ground for a predator whose methods were chillingly methodical and eerily consistent. This predator, later dubbed the "Monster of Florence," executed a series of gruesome murders that would leave an indelible scar on the region and its people.

The Monster's victims were couples seeking solace in each other's company, usually parked in secluded areas far from the prying eyes of civilization. Lovers found themselves ensnared by a false sense of security, lulled into vulnerability by the serenity of the countryside and the intimacy they shared. But where the night promised passion, it also concealed terror.

Under the cloak of darkness, the attacker bided his time, waiting for the perfect moment when the couple's attention was solely on each other. Then, like a specter emerging from the night's shadows, he would strike—swiftly and without hesitation. A gunshot would shatter the night's silence, its echoes marking the beginning of his deadly ritual. Both man and woman were shot, but the nightmare did not end there. The blade followed, a tool of both murder and macabre artistry.

It was with the knife that the Monster's true signature was carved—a grotesque ritual of disfigurement that spoke to a depravity beyond mere homicide. Particularly savage was his treatment of the female victims, whose bodies bore the marks of his twisted obsessions long after life had left them. This ritualistic aspect of his crimes became the grisly hallmark of his reign of terror.

The Monster operated on nights when the moon hid its face, as if nature itself conspired to keep his deeds secret. These were evenings chosen with care—nights preceding weekends or holidays, when the next day promised leisure rather than labor, ensuring more couples would venture out seeking escape under the stars.

Yet, the Monster was nothing if not strategic. Each new crime unfolded in a different section of the sprawling Florence suburbs, a constant relocation that kept authorities guessing and citizens in fear. His ability to shift locations with each attack added to the growing legend of his malevolence, a specter that haunted not just the darkened roads but the very psyche of a community.

In these moonless hours, the Monster of Florence etched his legacy into the walls of history, leaving behind a trail of blood and a city forever changed by his nocturnal horrors.

**The Victims:**

**Antonio Lo Bianco and Barbara Locci**

In the tranquil town of Signa, west of Florence, a horrifying murder would lay the groundwork for a series of chilling events. It was the night of August 21, 1968, when the tranquility of this small Italian town was shattered. In the quiet darkness, mason worker Antonio Lo Bianco, age 29, and homemaker Barbara Locci, age 32, were brutally gunned down in their car. The weapon—a .22 caliber handgun—spoke the language of death, leaving behind an ominous silence.

Lying asleep in the backseat was Locci's six-year-old son, Natalino Mele. Awakened by the aftermath, the young boy discovered his mother's lifeless form. In a state of pure terror, he fled into the night, eventually reaching the safety of a nearby house, his cries rousing the residents from their sleep.

Barbara Locci, originally from Sardinia, was known far and wide in the town. Her captivating presence earned her the nickname ape regina, or "Queen Bee." Yet, the title seemed to carry a sting. Her older husband, Stefano Mele, would soon find himself entangled in accusations, charged with orchestrating the murder of his wife. He would spend six years incarcerated, though the truth of those dark intentions remained elusive.

While Stefano languished behind bars, another couple fell victim, slain by what appeared to be the same elusive hand. Theories ran rampant through the tight-knit community. Whispers of Locci's numerous lovers being behind the murders echoed through the streets. Even Stefano himself voiced suspicions, suggesting that one of these men might have been the one to end Locci's life. Yet, as the pattern of killings continued even with these suspects imprisoned, the mystery only deepened.

Fast forward to 1982, when a mysterious letter from an anonymous writer—signing off as "Un cittadino amico" or "a friendly citizen"—brought the past back to light. The letter linked the brutal 1968 murders to more recent bloodshed. Magistrate Vincenzo Tricomi, upon reopening the dusty files of the forgotten case, uncovered a startling find —five bullets and shell casings, misplaced amidst Stefano Mele's cold case records.

What baffled investigators was the inexplicable presence of these pieces of evidence, suggesting a sinister connection between the old and new crimes. Yet, despite intense scrutiny, authorities failed to trace the chain of custody for these damning artifacts. They neglected a scientific comparison that could have unraveled the veiled history of the bullets. Their failure to uncover whether these cartridges matched the ballistic report from 1968 left a lingering question mark.

The link was clear to law enforcement, connecting the murderer of the recent double homicides with the shadowy figure behind the 1968 deaths. But without solid evidence, the phantom killer remained free to haunt the picturesque landscape of Florence, a specter of unresolved horror in the hearts of those left behind. In the annals of crime, the case of Lo Bianco and Locci serves as a poignant reminder of how evil can lurk quietly in the shadows, waiting for its moment to strike again.

### Pasquale Gentilcore and Stefania Pettini

On a seemingly ordinary night in September 1974, the tranquil countryside near Borgo San Lorenzo became the backdrop for a chilling crime that would haunt the region for years. Pasquale Gentilcore, a 19-year-old barman, and his girlfriend, 18-year-old accountant Stefania Pettini, had planned to spend a carefree evening at the Teen Club, a well-known discothèque, with friends. Instead, they found themselves in a secluded country lane, caught in a nightmare.

Gentilcore and Pettini were brutally attacked while in Gentilcore's Fiat 127. The young couple was not only shot but also viciously stabbed multiple times, their lives cut tragically short. Stefania's body bore the marks of an unspeakable violation—her wounds were etched into memory, with a grapevine stalk desecrating her remains, alongside 97 stab marks that spoke of a savage frenzy.

Unbeknownst to the couple, Stefania's fear was palpable days before their demise. She shared with a close friend her encounters with a disturbing presence—a man whose eerie behavior sent shivers down her spine. Another friend recounted a similar experience, a strange man shadowing them during a driving lesson, intensifying the unsettling aura surrounding Stefania's last days. The area, a known lovers' lane, was also frequented by peculiar voyeurs, adding yet another layer to the sinister mystery.

### Giovanni Foggi and Carmela De Nuccio

Fast forward to June 1981, when the quiet town of Scandicci became the scene of another horrific act. Giovanni Foggi, a 30-year-old warehouseman, and his fiancée Carmela De Nuccio, a 21-year-old shop assistant, fell victim to a brutal assault. Their lives were ended in a ruthless attack that mirrored the earlier tragedy.

The couple was found shot and stabbed, their dreams for the future forever shattered. Carmela's desecration was particularly gruesome—her body was dragged from the car, and her pubic area was grotesquely excised with a notched knife. The morning after, Enzo Spalletti, a young voyeur with a penchant for lurking in shadows, made the mistake of speaking about the crime before it became public knowledge. His premature commentary landed him in jail for three months, as suspicion clouded around him until the real perpetrator struck again, establishing a pattern that exonerated Spalletti.

### Stefano Baldi and Susanna Cambi

A mere four months later, in October 1981, the serene park near Calenzano bore witness to yet another dark chapter. Stefano Baldi, a 26-year-old workman, and his 24-year-old fiancée, Susanna Cambi, met a harrowing end. They were shot and stabbed in a chilling echo of past horrors. Susanna's body, like Carmela's, was mutilated in a manner that sent waves of terror through the community.

In a macabre twist, an anonymous caller tormented Susanna's mother the day after the murder, hinting at her daughter's fate. This callous act added to the anguish of Susanna's family, who were already aware of the mysterious figure that had been tormenting her, even pursuing her by car.

### Paolo Mainardi and Antonella Migliorini

In the shadowy recesses of Montespertoli's provincial roads, love and terror collided on the night of June 19, 1982. Amidst the gentle hum of a summer evening, mechanic Paolo Mainardi, 22, and dressmaker Antonella Migliorini, 20, sought privacy in what should have been a secluded sanctuary — the intimacy of a car. Yet, fate had a darker script.

Their clandestine rendezvous was abruptly interrupted as an unknown assailant shattered the tranquility with gunfire. Passersby, lured by the sudden illumination of the car's interior, caught fleeting glimpses of this tableau of horror. Mainardi, clinging to life, was rushed to the hospital. Despite heroic efforts, his injuries proved fatal.

Speculation has long swirled around those final moments. Some suggest Mainardi sensed the impending threat, desperately attempting to flee before veering into a ditch. Others propose a more haunting scenario, where the killer commandeered Mainardi's vehicle in a bid to conceal the crime, only to abandon it in haste. What is certain, however, is that the killer's trademark brutality was curtailed, leaving Migliorini unscathed by mutilation, not from mercy but from time's relentless march.

### Wilhelm Friedrich Horst Meyer and Jens Uwe Rüsch

A year later, on September 9, 1983, the killer struck again, targeting Wilhelm Friedrich Horst Meyer and Jens Uwe Rüsch, both 24, in the peaceful enclave of Galluzzo. These two German students, reveling in the joyous occasion of Meyer's scholarship win, sought solace within the confines of their Volkswagen Samba Bus.

The scene of their demise was one of jarring contrast — the vibrant promise of youth extinguished by a hail of bullets. Street whispers and investigative conjecture hinted at the possibility of mistaken identity. Rüsch's delicate features and flowing blond hair may have led the killer to mistakenly perceive him as female. Yet, the presence of explicit materials in their possession complicated the narrative, leading authorities to speculate about the nature of their relationship.

### Claudio Stefanacci and Pia Gilda Rontini

The killer's malevolent path carved its way into the lives of Claudio Stefanacci and Pia Gilda Rontini on July 29, 1984. Parked in the seclusion of a woodland near Vicchio, the law student and barmaid became the latest victims in a gruesome series. Stefano, 21, and Rontini, 18, met a violent end, their bodies marked by both gunshots and knife wounds.

Rontini endured the cruelest fate, her body desecrated with surgical precision. The community whispered of a sinister figure seen trailing the couple earlier that day at an ice cream parlor. Friends recall Pia's unease, confiding in them about a disturbing presence that haunted her workplace. This ominous figure now seemed to cast a long shadow over their tragic end.

### Jean Michel Kraveichvili and Nadine Mauriot

The killer's final act unfolded under the canopy of San Casciano's woods during the night of September 7–8, 1985. Jean Michel Kraveichvili, a 25-year-old musician of Georgian descent, and Nadine Mauriot, aged 36, were ambushed as they sought refuge in a small tent. Their French origins rendered them invisible to local authorities, no warning signs heralding their disappearance.

Kraveichvili made a desperate bid for survival, his life extinguished just beyond the tent's flimsy fabric. Mauriot's lifeless form bore the chilling signature of mutilation. In a macabre twist, the killer taunted the authorities, dispatching a piece of Mauriot's breast alongside a chilling note to State Prosecutor Silvia Della Monica. The bodies, concealed by the woodland's verdant cloak, remained undiscovered until a mushroom gatherer unearthed their grisly secret, mere hours before the killer's taunt reached Della Monica's desk.

These acts of calculated brutality, each more audacious than the last, left an indelible mark on the landscape of Florence. The killer's identity remains shrouded in mystery, a specter lurking in the shadows. The victims' stories endure, haunting reminders of innocence lost and the relentless pursuit of justice.

## The Enigma of the Monster of Florence

The quiet streets of Florence were not accustomed to the kind of unease that now lingered in their corners. In the hunt for a shadowy figure known as the Monster of Florence, investigators faced one of Italy's most chilling mysteries. At the heart of this case lay not just a series of brutal murders, but a mind that eluded understanding—a predator whose very existence seemed to defy the complacency of everyday life.

To catch a killer, one must first understand him. Italian authorities called upon Francesco de Fazio, an esteemed criminologist from Modena, to unravel the psyche of this elusive murderer. De Fazio painted a portrait of a lone wolf, a man who roamed society's peripheries, a bachelor disconnected from intimacy and companionship.

His solitude was telling, as was his impotence—a condition implied by the absence of sexual acts at the crime scenes, save for the grisly violation of the first victim with an olive branch. This lack of physical connection to his crimes suggested an individual whose excitement stemmed solely from the act of killing itself—a lust murderer.

Believed to be around 40 years old in 1985, this man likely favored the intimacy of a knife over the detachment of a gun, savoring the visceral thrill it provided. His restless nature was mirrored in his unstable employment, never settling long enough to be tied down by routine.

The scope of the Monster of Florence's menace necessitated international assistance, bringing the FBI into the fold. From across the Atlantic, American profilers offered their insights, corroborating and expanding upon existing theories. They envisioned a man slightly older, possibly around 45, forged in the earthy resilience of manual labor.

Not one for intellectual pursuits, his intelligence was deemed average, and his personal life mirrored his professional one—solitary and barren of romantic entanglements. This bachelor's lair was likely near the site of his inaugural crime, a place where he could retreat unnoticed, perhaps sharing a roof with an elderly relative to maintain a veneer of normalcy.

The lack of female companionship pointed towards deeper issues, perhaps a sexual dysfunction that drove him to seek fulfillment through more sinister means. Drugs or alcohol may have served as his companions in crime, dulling any inhibitions as he prepared for his nocturnal hunts.

This intricate profile was a tapestry woven from fragments of evidence and intuition. It served as both a beacon and a warning, illuminating the path of investigation while reminding the world of the monstrous potential hidden within ordinary façades. The Monster of Florence remained a chilling enigma, his true face obscured by the shadows in which he thrived.

### Why Was the Monster of Florence So Elusive?

From the chilling double murder in 1974 to the last known crime in 1985, the Monster of Florence haunted the Italian countryside, leaving authorities baffled. Despite the concentrated efforts of law enforcement, the elusive killer always seemed one step ahead. But why was this predator so difficult to capture?

In 1985, a seasoned magistrate, Francesco Fleury, pondered this very question. When asked about the challenges in apprehending the killer, Fleury elaborated on the unique difficulties posed by the Mostro.

The first hurdle? Solitude. Unlike many criminals who operate within a network or with accomplices, the Mostro acted alone. This solitude made it incredibly challenging to pinpoint any loose ends that might traditionally lead to a suspect's capture.

Furthermore, there was a chilling randomness to his choice of victims. The Mostro had no known connection to those he killed, rendering traditional motives like revenge or jealousy moot. These victims were selected seemingly at random, making it a Herculean task to predict or prevent the next attack.

His attacks were swift and meticulous—an orchestrated dance of death that took less than ten minutes. This efficiency left little room for error, and even less room for evidence. Once he vanished into the night, he remained a ghost for what often felt like an eternity.

Adding to the complexity was the vast territory in which the Monster operated. The sprawling countryside around Florence provided the perfect stage for his deadly performances. The dark, wooded areas offered natural cover, making surveillance nearly impossible.

Maurizio Cimmino, an esteemed police investigator, offered further insights into the investigation's challenges. The

Mostro's strategy was flawless; he struck under the cover of night, ensuring privacy. No witnesses ever emerged, as though the killer had conducted an invisible census of each location, confirming it was free of prying eyes.

To complicate matters, the motives behind these gruesome acts were inscrutable. Unlike crimes driven by passion or profit, there was no thread of logic for investigators to tug on.

Initially, the police followed conventional investigative paths, probing into the lives of the victims and interrogating old flames. But these familiar strategies proved futile against a criminal mind that defied standard profiling.

Italy's law enforcement was adept at handling crimes of passion or untangling the intricate webs of mafia-related cases. Yet, they were ill-prepared to confront a serial killer —the likes of whom they'd never encountered before. This unfamiliar terrain highlighted a significant gap in their expertise.

The enigma of the Monster of Florence serves as a haunting reminder of how a single individual, armed with cunning and patience, can confound even the most seasoned investigators. And thus, a chapter in true crime remains open, inviting us to ponder the perennial question —how does one catch a ghost?

## Investigation and Suspects

It wasn't until the chilling Foggi-De Nuccio murders of 1981 that investigators realized the same sinister hand was behind these heinous acts. A 1974 newspaper article linking the Gentilcore-Pettini murder prompted authorities to perform ballistics tests, revealing a disturbing truth—the same weapon had been used. This revelation led reporter Mario Spezi to christen the culprit as the ominous "Monster of Florence."

### The Sardinian Connection

In the aftermath of 1982, a calculated move by law enforcement leaked false news that victim Mainardi had regained consciousness before succumbing to his injuries. This deceptive tactic led to an anonymous tip urging a fresh look at the unsolved Lo Bianco-Locci murder from 1968. Once again, the same firearm emerged as the silent witness to these crimes, casting doubt on the confession of Stefano Mele, who was behind bars during subsequent murders.

The investigative maze unraveled further when Francesco Vinci, a former lover of Locci, found himself ensnared in the spotlight. His car's suspicious disappearance on the day of the false information leak added fuel to the fire. Despite being detained for over a year, the murders persisted. The hunt widened; Francesco's brother Salvatore—whose own past was shadowed by the mysterious "suicide" of his wife—became another focal point. Yet, the final act of the Monster in 1985 proved the Vinci brothers' innocence as they languished in custody.

## The "Snack Buddies"

The murky waters of investigation turned toward Pietro Pacciani, a man with a dark past of rape and murder. His life bore eerie parallels to the Monster's modus operandi. Inspector Ruggero Perugini zeroed in on Pacciani, unearthing a treasure trove of incriminating material, including an unfired bullet tied to the Monster's rampage. Yet, the bullet was a plant.

Pacciani's initial conviction in 1994 sparked controversy and, after a successful appeal highlighting lackluster police work, he was freed in 1996. However, the Supreme Court demanded a retrial, but fate intervened; Pacciani died in 1998, leaving unanswered questions.

Pacciani's so-called "Snack Buddy," Mario Vanni, professed their innocence, claiming they simply shared meals together—a phrase that became infamous in the Italian lexicon. Yet, Lotti, a surprise witness, claimed to have seen Pacciani and Vanni in the act. Amidst multiple confessions, he even implicated himself. Despite convictions, many critics remain unconvinced, leaving the case unresolved.

## The Satanic Cult Theory

By 2001, the narrative took a mystic turn. Chief inspector Michele Giuttari posited that the murders were the work of a sinister satanic cult rooted in Florence. An alleged doctor, Pacciani's employer, was rumored to have orchestrated the killings, harvesting victims' genitalia for ritualistic purposes. The theory gained traction with the discovery of a stone near Pacciani's workplace, claimed to be a cult marker.

Skeptics, however, dismissed it as mere folklore, pointing to the mundane use of such stones as doorstops.

The allure of riches further complicated matters. Pacciani, once a simple farmer, had amassed considerable wealth during the crime spree, fueling speculation of shadowy backers. Despite investigations, the theory of a clandestine order directing the "Snack Buddies" faltered, and no further leads emerged.

In 2010, the seasoned prosecutor Pier Luigi Vigna expressed doubt about these esoteric claims, a sentiment echoed by the fruitless inquiries that followed. The Monster of Florence remains a haunting mystery, echoing through the annals of unsolved crimes—a puzzle still awaiting its final piece.

## The Doctor and the Secret Society

The mystery surrounding the Monster of Florence was steeped in secrecy and suspicion, with whispers of secret societies and hidden motives echoing through the corridors of power. At the center of this tangled web was a chilling theory involving two seemingly respectable figures – a pharmacist named Francesco Calamandrei and the late physician Francesco Narducci.

Lotti's unsettling testimony hinted at a doctor's involvement in orchestrating the sinister events that haunted Florence. This ignited the imaginations of investigators like Chief Inspector Michele Giuttari and the tenacious prosecutor of Perugia, Giuliano Mignini. Gabriella Carlizzi, the astute editor-in-chief of L'Altra Repubblica, joined forces with them to unravel the potential connections between these men and a shadowy secret society.

Francesco Narducci, a promising young doctor from an esteemed Perugian family, vanished mysteriously while sailing on Lake Trasimeno. His body surfaced days later, on October 13, 1985, just a month after the Monster's latest gruesome act. The method of identification and the speed of his burial fueled speculation, especially in the eyes of the determined Magistrate Mignini. In a twist that seemed plucked from the pages of a thriller, intercepted phone calls during an anti-usury probe hinted at ties between Narducci, the Monster, and a dark cult.

The Perugia Public Prosecutor's Office began to entertain a chilling hypothesis—could Narducci's identity have been swapped with another victim? Could his death have been more malevolent than an accidental drowning? When his body was exhumed in 2002, forensic experts found signs consistent with strangulation—a stark contradiction to the initial reports citing drowning as the cause of death. This revelation cast a shadow of doubt over the Narducci family and their supposed role in covering up a crime more insidious than previously imagined.

Legal battles ensued, dragging Narducci's friend, the lawyer Alfredo Brizioli, into the fray. Accusations flew, alleging he pressured a medical examiner to falsify Narducci's autopsy report. Yet, in a dramatic courtroom climax, the Supreme Court cleared the family of all charges, as well as Calamandrei of any wrongdoing.

During this tumultuous period, journalist Mario Spezi found himself in Mignini's crosshairs. Accused of meddling in the investigation, Spezi was arrested amidst claims of his allegiance to the same nefarious sect being probed. An international uproar ensued, leading to Spezi's release and the collapse of the case against him.

Amidst the chaos, both Giuttari and Mignini faced legal scrutiny for their handling of the investigation, culminating in the disbandment of GIDES, the task force dedicated to solving the Monster of Florence case.

Yet, as with any gripping saga, the story refused to fade into obscurity. In 2018, the specter of Narducci's alleged involvement in the Monster's killings emerged once more, linked to the mysterious disappearance of Rossella Corazzin in Belluno in 1975. The Bicameral Anti-Mafia Parliamentary Commission suggested that the puzzle remained incomplete, hinting that this dark chapter was deserving of further exploration.

## The Zodiac Killer

In 2017, Francesco Amicone, a tenacious freelance journalist, embarked on a quest that would take him down a chilling path connecting two of history's most infamous serial killers—the Zodiac Killer and the Monster of Florence. His investigation, which has captured the attention of true crime aficionados, unraveled a thread that leads to one man—Joseph Bevilacqua.

Bevilacqua, also known as Giuseppe, was a former superintendent at the Florence American Cemetery in Italy. His legacy was not one of peace, but rather one cloaked in suspicion. The tale takes a dark turn when we discover Bevilacqua's extensive military career, which saw him retire to Florence in 1974 under mysterious circumstances.

Amicone's relentless pursuit led to an intense series of seven meetings with Bevilacqua, each lasting hours and meticulously scrutinized by the Florence ROS Carabinieri in 2018. During a pivotal phone call on September 12, 2017, Bevilacqua whispered confessions that sent shivers down the spine—hinting at his involvement in both the Zodiac and the Monster cases. Yet, like a ghost, he retracted his confession, leaving no recorded trace behind.

In these secret meetings, Bevilacqua divulged that he had served as an undercover CID investigator in California during the Zodiac's reign of terror. He was part of the investigation into the notorious "Khaki Mafia," a shadowy group operating in the murky underworld of military corruption.

In 2018, Amicone bravely published his findings, sparking a media frenzy across Italy and beyond. Despite Bevilacqua's vehement denials and subsequent legal battles, the journalist stood firm, unyielding in his accusations.

One of Amicone's most startling assertions was the possibility that Bevilacqua had tampered with evidence from a 1968 double murder near Florence. He suggested that Bevilacqua might have cunningly replaced bullets and shell casings with those fired by his own gun, plotting to connect his future crimes with a murder for which he had a solid alibi.

Even more intriguing is the fact that Bevilacqua was stationed in Vietnam in 1968, but Amicone speculated that he had access to trial files where evidence was improperly handled. According to a detailed report submitted by Amicone in 2021, interviews with ballistics experts hinted that the evidence from the Monster's gun may not match the original 1968 casings.

Despite Amicone's tireless efforts, the investigation into Bevilacqua's potential involvement was dismissed in 2021, leading to the journalist being charged with defamation. Yet, in November 2023, Amicone made a bold move by sending Bevilacqua's DNA profile to American authorities investigating the Zodiac case.

This twist-laden saga unfolds with the tension and intrigue reminiscent of a noir thriller. The question remains—could Bevilacqua be the sinister connection between these two legendary cases, or is he merely a pawn in a much larger game of shadows? The truth may lie just beneath the surface, waiting to be uncovered.

Decades have passed, yet the chilling tale of the "Mostro di Firenze" continues to captivate the imagination of true crime enthusiasts and mystery lovers alike. The intrigue surrounding this elusive figure shows no signs of fading; instead, it grows stronger with each passing year. Books continue to be penned, online forums abuzz with speculation, and filmmakers pour their creative energies into television movies and documentaries, all seeking to unravel the enigma that haunts the Tuscan landscape.

In 2013, Florence played host to the 'First National Convention on the Monster of Florence,' a gathering that brought together a myriad of individuals—detectives, lawyers, and journalists—who had been deeply entrenched in the investigations and subsequent court proceedings. Their attendance was a testament to the enduring fascination and unresolved questions that hover like a shadow over this case.

The convictions of Pietro Pacciani, Mario Vanni, and Giancarlo Lotti have done little to satisfy the public's thirst for answers. To this day, the question lingers—"Who was – or *who is* - the Monster of Florence?" In truth, the identity of this malevolent figure remains as elusive as the shadows he once prowled. With every new revelation, the mystery deepens, ensuring that the story of the Mostro di Firenze will remain etched in the annals of true crime for years to come.

# CHAPTER FOURTEEN

## WHO WAS JENNIFER FAIRGATE?

In the summer of 1995, amidst the elegance of Oslo's prestigious Plaza Hotel, a mystery unfolded that would perplex investigators and intrigue the public for decades. The saga began with a woman known only as "Jennifer Fairgate," whose mysterious death in an upscale suite was cloaked in ambiguity. What appeared to be a straightforward suicide unraveled into a labyrinth of unanswered questions, suggesting a more sinister plot. With a fabricated identity, and a string of bizarre inconsistencies, her story whispers of espionage and international concealment. Despite exhaustive investigations and exhumation efforts, her identity remains elusive, casting shadows on a tale that captivates with the chilling allure of an unsolved mystery, forever etched in the annals of conspiracy and intrigue.

---

## The Mystery at Oslo Plaza

On a warm evening in June 1995, the serene atmosphere of the Oslo Plaza Hotel was shattered by a tragic discovery in Room 2805. Inside, a woman lay lifeless on the bed, a Browning 9 mm pistol precariously in her right hand, her thumb still pressing against the trigger. A single bullet had pierced her forehead, suggesting a seemingly straightforward suicide. However, upon closer inspection, the scene unveiled a labyrinth of questions and uncertainties.

The woman's identity was an enigma, cloaked in deliberate mystery. She checked into the hotel under a false name, paid in cash, and left no traceable documents behind. Every piece of clothing in the room had its labels meticulously removed, and even the gun's serial numbers were filed off, leaving investigators with nothing to grasp onto. It was as if she wanted to vanish from existence, leaving the world with no breadcrumbs to follow.

Yet, one item stood untouched by her fervent attempts to erase her identity—a Citizen Aqualand watch on her left wrist. This wasn't just any watch; it was a rugged, military-grade timepiece. Known for its durability and association with elite military units like the British Special Boat Service and the Danish Frogman Corps, the Aqualand was an unusual choice for a woman of apparent Belgian descent with a flair for fashion. Its presence added another layer of intrigue to an already perplexing case.

The mystery of Room 2805 beckons with questions that remain unanswered. Who was this woman? What drove her to such lengths to hide her identity? And why did she leave only a singular clue in the form of an incongruous watch?

It's been nearly thirty years since the mysterious death of the woman known only as "Jennifer Fairgate," yet the circumstances surrounding her demise continue to baffle investigators. Her story unfolds like a suspenseful thriller, with each turn of events more bewildering than the last.

Was Jennifer Fairgate caught in the crosshairs of high-stakes espionage? Theories abound, fueled by Hollywood's portrayal of shadowy intelligence operations. Some dare to speculate that she might have been an operative or even an assassin, but the truth remains elusive.

The case is riddled with more questions than answers, each clue leading to a maze of dead ends. One intriguing aspect of her story is the Citizen watch she wore at the time of her death. Could this timepiece hold the key to unlocking her identity and uncovering her trade?

Initial reports hinted that Jennifer Fairgate wasn't alone. A man named "Lois Fairgate" – Lois is a more common male name in Europe than in the U.S. - was later linked to the room registration, though his existence remains as puzzling as the alias itself. Upon registration, 'Jennifer' listed a fictitious address in Belgium and claimed to be 21 years old. Forensic experts, however, would later estimate her age closer to 30. This discrepancy, along with her fabricated identity, adds mysterious layers to her story.

The Netflix series *Unsolved Mysteries* cast a spotlight on Jennifer's peculiar behavior. For days, she remained secluded behind a 'Do Not Disturb' sign, her activities unknown.

On June 3rd, just days after her arrival, the narrative took a dark turn. Hotel staff approached room 2805, seeking payment from the elusive Fairgate. Suddenly, a gunshot reverberated from within. The startled employee fled to summon the head of security, leaving the room unwatched for fifteen critical minutes. Upon their return, they found the door locked from the inside. Once they gained entry, the acrid scent of gunpowder lingered in the air, a grim indicator of the recent firearm discharge. Inside, Jennifer lay lifeless on the bed, her shoes still on.

At first glance, it seemed a tragic end—a woman perhaps overwhelmed by the weight of despair. However, whispers of espionage and secret affairs soon swirled around her death. Was she a spy, drawn into a deadly game of international intrigue? Or an assassin, silenced after a mission gone awry? Ola Kaldager, a former Norwegian Intelligence Service officer, suggested a more sinister narrative. He theorized that Jennifer was indeed an intelligence operative, and her death was artfully staged to mimic suicide. Yet, Kaldager was convinced it was an execution, a cold calculation disguised as self-destruction.

In the shadowy world of espionage, the simplest details often carry the heaviest weight. The case of Fairgate, an enigmatic figure whose presence was as elusive as her past, raises questions that beckon even the most seasoned sleuths. Could she have been more than just a mysterious guest at the hotel where our story unfolds?

Fairgate's profile aligns suspiciously well with that of an intelligence officer. Hotels have long been the silent stage for espionage activities, offering anonymity amidst the hustle and bustle. Despite the increasing challenges posed by pervasive surveillance technology, these venues remain a staple in the spy's toolkit. Fairgate's extended absences—one spanning an intriguing 20 hours—hint at activities beyond those of an ordinary traveler.

Intriguingly, logs from the hotel's keycard reader reveal these prolonged periods of absence. Such disappearances could suggest operational endeavors, akin to the covert maneuvers employed by CIA operatives. They often exploit similar strategies, using hotels as meeting points and adopting temporary identities, or "throwaway aliases," to mask their true intentions.

A deeper investigation into Fairgate's room unveiled a spartan collection of personal effects, with one exception—a surprisingly extensive array of clothing options for her upper body. Sweaters and trench coats lined her closet, perhaps intended for swift transformations and concealment during covert operations. While the removal of clothing tags isn't standard practice, intelligence agents are rigorously trained to eliminate any form of identification or "pocket litter" when assuming an alias.

The mystery of Fairgate deepens with every detail uncovered. Her strategic absences and meticulously curated wardrobe point to a life lived in the shadows, where every choice is deliberate and every move calculated.

Was it a calculated assassination or a tragic case of suicide? An atmosphere of uncertainty filled the room where "Jennifer" met her mysterious fate.

The mystery began with an eerie 15-minute silence that followed the deafening crack of a gunshot. By the time hotel security arrived, the room was sealed from the inside, a feat that could suggest the work of a skilled professional making a swift exit.

Investigators scrutinized the scene, uncovering peculiar details that cast doubt on the suicide theory. The pistol Jennifer supposedly used was found with an awkward grip, raising suspicions. Even more telling, there was no trace of blood spatter on Jennifer's hand, prompting questions about a possible second shooter.

Adding to the intrigue, a second bullet hole pierced through a pillow and embedded itself in the mattress below. Was this a deliberate warning shot, aimed at deterring a hotel attendant who dared approach the door? Or perhaps a test shot fired in preparation for a more sinister act?

Theories abounded, each more captivating than the last. Historians and intelligence analysts noted a chilling connection to the dark arts of espionage. Intelligence agencies like the Russian KGB/FSB and Israeli Mossad have long been suspected of orchestrating assassinations disguised as suicides. Both organizations have a documented history of operating in Norway, fueling speculation that Jennifer's death could have been a meticulously planned hit.

These tantalizing clues and the veil of secrecy they shrouded made for a compelling puzzle.

### The Enigma of the Watch

In the intriguing world of espionage and mystery, every detail counts. The seemingly ordinary can reveal extraordinary secrets, as is the case with the watch the victim was wearing. The Citizen Aqualand diver's watch, a sturdy timepiece crafted for underwater missions, isn't just a mere accessory—it's a sophisticated device equipped with a depth gauge and a no-decompression limit (NDL) chart emblazoned on the strap. In the realm of tool watches, the Aqualand stands supreme, purpose-built for secrecy and precision.

This particular watch model is no stranger to elite maritime units across Europe. From the Italian Navy to the UK's Special Operations, and most notably, the Danish Frogman Corps (Frømandskorpset), the Citizen Aqualand has found its way onto the wrists of these covert operatives. Its connection to the Danish Frogman Corps is particularly compelling given its proximity to Norway, where the mysterious "Jennifer" was discovered.

While the presence of this watch alone does not imply direct involvement with intelligence agencies, it is far from a common choice—especially when juxtaposed with the stylish but mainstream wardrobe found with the woman. A robust watch like this is indispensable in the world of espionage, where its dual analog/digital capabilities prove invaluable. In the 1990s, real divers swore by the Aqualand, as noted by Jason Heaton, a fellow diver who observed that this model was "the last true diver's watch designed and acquired by genuine divers." Could Jennifer have been a diver, or was there a deeper connection?

To decipher the story behind the watch, we must trace its history beyond its surface allure.

An investigative piece by the Norwegian newspaper VG unearthed some fascinating details about this particular Citizen Aqualand, reference CQ-1021-50. According to their findings, it rolled off production lines in January 1992, bearing the serial number C022-088093 Y, 2010779, GN-4-S. Citizen in Japan corroborated these details. Upon closer examination, investigators uncovered three Swiss-made Renata 370-type batteries inside, marked with "W395," suggesting they were installed in March 1995; the "W" potentially pointing to the initials of the watchmaker.

Some suggest the watch was bought in Germany, but no concrete evidence substantiates this theory. It was eventually auctioned off at a police sale. Notably, watchmakers traditionally engrave discreet notes on either the inner caseback or, as in this case, directly onto the battery. These markings serve as a historical record, offering insights into its maintenance history for future horologists.

While the watch itself might not conclusively identify Jennifer as an intelligence officer, it offers tantalizing clues. Its military ties and specialized features add layers to the mystery that beg further exploration. Could this watch be the key to unlocking more of Jennifer's true identity, or simply a red herring in the complex tapestry of her life?

**A Wilderness of Mirrors**

The intelligence community is often described as a "wilderness of mirrors," a world where truths are elusive and appearances deceptive. This murky realm was the focus of a fascinating interview conducted by the online blog, "Watches of Espionage," with John Sipher, a former CIA officer who once led operations in Russia. His insights shed light on the complex interplay between espionage and organized crime, particularly in the context of Norway and other Scandinavian countries.

Sipher, who also served in Nordic regions during the turbulent 1990s, explained that countries like Norway have long been strategic focal points for Russia. Factors such as proximity, the criticality of the Baltic Sea, and access to Western Europe make these regions especially important. This interest was underscored in October 2022 when Norway's domestic security agency apprehended Mikhail Mikushin, suspected of being a Russian GRU operative disguised as a Brazilian academic named José Assis Giammaria.

Amidst these unfolding events, Sipher speculated on the enigmatic figure known only as Jennifer Fairgate. Could she have been a Russian intelligence officer or asset? Or perhaps her connections lay within the shadows of organized crime? Sipher noted that in the tangled world of the 1990s, these affiliations were often intertwined.

**Russian Organized Crime**

In the chaotic aftermath of the Soviet Union's collapse, a cohort of former KGB officers found new allegiances within the burgeoning networks of organized crime. These "formers" possessed unique skills, adept at navigating international banking systems and executing tasks across Europe. According to Sipher, there was a significant overlap between Russian organized crime and intelligence operations, with each seamlessly blending into the other.

Former CIA Director James Woolsey famously warned, "If you meet an articulate Russian in a $3,000 suit claiming to be an executive, he might be telling the truth—or he might be part of Russian intelligence, organized crime, or perhaps even both. In this world, such affiliations aren't mutually exclusive."

While Fairgate's profile might align with that of a Russian operative, the direct evidence connecting her to Russia remains elusive.

Sipher also highlighted the post-unification shifts in Germany, where former East German intelligence officers, once part of the feared Stasi, found themselves at crossroads. Many leveraged their skills to collaborate with Russian services or criminal networks. These seasoned operatives, familiar with Soviet techniques, could travel across Europe with little suspicion.

Some evidence points towards Fairgate's possible connection to East Germany—her accent, certain forensic DNA findings, and items like her watch originating from Germany. Could she have been an ex-Stasi agent working under a new guise?

**Mossad and The Oslo Accords**

The Oslo Plaza Hotel, another piece of the puzzle, was reportedly a backdrop for clandestine negotiations between Israel and Palestinian authorities leading up to the Oslo II Accord. Was Fairgate linked to these high-stakes discussions? Could she have been an Israeli agent or perhaps the victim of a Mossad operation?

Mossad is renowned for its covert operations and targeted eliminations. The infamous 2010 assassination of a Hamas official in Dubai and the botched 1973 Lillehammer Affair in Norway underscore their lethal efficiency and occasional missteps. While no direct ties link Fairgate to Israeli operations, Mossad's use of dual-citizens for clandestine missions keeps the door open to possibilities.

Though connections between Fairgate and the Israeli Defense Forces or Mossad-issued watches remain speculative, the intrigue of her story lies in these potential intersections of espionage and subterfuge.

**The Mystery Lingers On**

In this labyrinth of deception and danger, the truth about Fairgate remains as elusive as a shadow on a moonlit night —a testament to the wilderness of mirrors that is the world of espionage and crime.

The enigma surrounding the woman known as "Jennifer Fairgate" remains tantalizingly unsolved, leaving us with a myriad of questions and hypotheses. Her story is shrouded in mystery, with anomalies that hint at a possible life steeped in espionage. Yet, the truth could be as mundane as it is intriguing—perhaps she was tangled in illicit activities or lived under the guise of an escort. Espionage, often dubbed the "world's second oldest profession," shares an uncanny resemblance to the first, and her mysterious existence might have woven threads from both worlds.

The portrayal of intelligence work in Hollywood is often larger than life, filled with dramatic plots and nail-biting suspense. In reality, while such high-stakes operations do occur, the daily grind of espionage is far less glamorous. With operations cloaked in secrecy and outcomes often ambiguous, the true picture of Jennifer's involvement is blurred, like a puzzle missing critical pieces. What we grasp is a mere fragment of a larger story, perhaps not even its conclusion.

Could this have been a covert mission orchestrated by the Russians, Israelis, or another shadowy organization? Or was it a desperate attempt by a woman to vanish without a trace, crafting her own escape from reality? If the latter is true, she succeeded in her vanishing act with chilling precision.

Amidst the uncertainty, one clue stubbornly lingers—the watch on her wrist. This seemingly inconspicuous timepiece may hold the key to unraveling her identity. Somewhere, hidden in the bustling chaos of a watchmaker's workshop, may lie the answer to this mystery. This watch stands as a testament to the notion that sometimes, the smallest object can illuminate the darkest obscurities, inviting us all to ponder the question—who was Jennifer Fairgate, and what secrets did she carry with her to the grave?

# CHAPTER FIFTEEN

## WHAT HAPPENED TO THE JAMISON FAMILY?

On a quiet day in October 2009, the Jamison family vanished from their home in Eufaula, Oklahoma, leaving behind a trail of puzzling clues but few answers. Bobby Dale Jamison, his wife Sherilynn, and their six-year-old daughter, Madyson, seemed to lead an ordinary life in their rural community. Yet, on October 8, they disappeared without a trace, sparking one of the most perplexing mysteries in recent history.

The search for the Jamisons began with urgency, but as the days stretched on, it yielded more confusion than clarity. Not long after their disappearance, authorities discovered the family's abandoned pickup truck in a remote area. Inside, investigators found the Jamisons' belongings, including their IDs, wallets, and a considerable amount of cash—an unusual find that only deepened the mystery surrounding their fate. The vehicle's presence in such an isolated location prompted a multitude of theories, ranging from foul play to voluntary disappearance.

Despite an exhaustive search effort, the mystery endured for years until November 2013, when the skeletal remains of Bobby, Sherilynn, and Madyson were discovered in a rural part of Latimer County, less than four miles from where their truck had been found. Unfortunately, the passage of time and the condition of the remains left investigators with more questions than answers, and the case remains unsolved to this day.

How could a seemingly ordinary family vanish so completely, only to be found years later so close to their last known location? Were they victims of a sinister plot, or did they meet their fate by some tragic accident? These are the questions that continue to haunt those who have followed the case.

---

On an ordinary day in early October 2009, the Jamison family—Bobby, Sherilynn, and their six-year-old daughter, Madyson—vanished without a trace. Residents of Eufaula, Oklahoma, the family was reportedly scouting a 40-acre plot near Red Oak, a mere 30 miles from their home, with hopes of starting a new life. They intended to convert a storage container into their living quarters—a vision as unconventional as the circumstances surrounding their disappearance.

The last known sighting of the family was on October 8, by a local man who lived in the mountainous region of southeastern Oklahoma. He reported seeing the family, but no one else, adding to the mystery that would soon unravel.

Eight days passed before the first significant discovery was made. Hunters stumbled upon the Jamison family's abandoned truck, locked and eerily undisturbed, a mere quarter-mile from their last known location. Inside the vehicle were Bobby's wallet, Sherilynn's purse, jackets, a GPS device, and a substantial $32,000 cash hidden under the driver's seat. Their malnourished dog, Maisie, was found alive but barely clinging to life. Bobby's cell phone was also left behind, containing a photo of young Madyson, assumed to be taken the day before their disappearance. Curiously, there were no signs of a struggle in or around the truck.

Former Latimer County Sheriff Israel Beauchamp suggested a chilling theory, "I think they were forced to stop and got out of the truck to meet with someone they recognize. And I think they either left willingly or by force."

The GPS data revealed that the family had ventured further up a nearby hill before returning to the truck's location. Investigators followed the coordinates and discovered footprints, sparking a large-scale search operation involving over 300 people. However, despite these efforts, the trail went cold, and hope for finding the family alive began to dwindle.

Fast forward to November 2013, when deer hunters, traversing the dense woods less than three miles from where the Jamisons vanished, uncovered skeletal remains of two adults and a child. The discovery of shoes, clothing scraps, teeth, and bone fragments confirmed the community's worst fears. After nearly four years, the Jamison family had been found, though only partially, their story still shrouded in mystery.

Dr. Joshua Lanter, the state medical examiner, faced the daunting task of identifying a cause of death. The incomplete state of the remains made this nearly impossible. There were no clear signs of trauma, yet it couldn't be entirely ruled out. Post-mortem damage caused by animals erased vital details. Ultimately, Dr. Lanter concluded that the deaths occurred under suspicious circumstances.

Adding to the intrigue, two items were notably absent from the discovery site—a briefcase and a .22 caliber handgun registered to Sherilynn. Both remain missing to this day. Financially, the Jamisons were living off disability checks, with Bobby incapacitated by an accident. Yet, the origin of the $32,000 remains a mystery, with Sherilynn's mother, Connie Kokotan, expressing ignorance regarding any settlement.

A further puzzle was presented by security footage from the Jamison home, dated the day they left. The video, reviewed by investigators, depicted the couple moving between their home and truck in a trance-like state, as if performing an unwritten ritual. They moved silently and methodically, occasionally pausing to stare into the distance—a haunting image that refuses to fade.

Sheriff Beauchamp reflected on the baffling nature of the case, stating, "Normally you can go through an investigation and one by one, start to eliminate certain scenarios. We haven't been able to do that in this case. With this family, everything seems possible."

The Jamison family's disappearance and subsequent discovery raise more questions than answers, leaving a perplexing riddle that time has yet to solve.

**Disappearance**

It was the kind of mystery that sent shivers down the spine of seasoned investigators. The Jamison family—Bobby, Sherilynn, and their six-year-old daughter Madyson—seemingly vanished into thin air.

Their disappearance began unraveling when their pickup truck was discovered in the remote, wooded area of Latimer County, Oklahoma. It sat abandoned just south of the small town of Kinta, a silent witness to the macabre mystery that had unfolded. Inside the vehicle, investigators found a scene that was both perplexing and deeply unsettling. The family's dog, Maisie, was left malnourished but alive, hinting at the duration of their absence. Yet, the Jamisons themselves were nowhere to be found.

Among the possessions left behind were items that painted a picture as puzzling as it was ominous. ID cards, wallets, mobile phones, a GPS system, and an astonishing $32,000 in cash were all present in the vehicle—an unusual detail for a family not known for carrying large sums of money. Why would they leave without their mobile phones? Did they plan on being gone only briefly? Why did they need a GPS system and so much money? Did they plan on going off the grid? These findings only deepened the enigma surrounding their vanishing act.

Adding an eerie layer to the case, home surveillance footage captured the Jamisons on the day they departed.

The video revealed the couple making several trips between their house and their vehicle. Their movements, devoid of speech and marked by a strange, almost hypnotic rhythm, were described by some as "trancelike." In the footage, Sherilynn was seen placing a brown briefcase into the vehicle—a briefcase that, along with her handgun, has never been recovered.

Former Sheriff Beauchamp speculated that the briefcase might hold a crucial piece of the puzzle. Yet, despite extensive searches and investigations, what exactly it contained remains one of the many secrets the Jamisons took with them.

**Discovery**

In the dense and untamed wilderness of Latimer County, Oklahoma, a grim discovery awaited two unsuspecting hunters on a crisp November day in 2013. It had been over four long years since the Jamison family vanished without a trace, leaving behind a trail of questions and a community gripped by mystery.

The hunters had ventured into a remote, rarely traversed area, their attention absorbed by the promise of game. But what they stumbled upon was far from the usual forest finds—skeletal remains scattered across the cool forest floor. Chillingly, these remnants belonged to two adults and a child, evoking a somber silence amidst the trees.

Just under three miles away, the family's pickup truck had been found abandoned years prior, stirring speculation and unending theories. Yet now, with the discovery of these bones, the whispers of the past grew louder. The widespread belief that these were the remains of the Jamison family was almost unanimous, casting a shadow of finality over their disappearances.

The identification of the bodies, however, was not immediate. Nature had reclaimed much, leaving the remains heavily decomposed and challenging to analyze. It required the meticulous work of forensic experts, who employed anthropological and pathological techniques to unlock the secrets the bodies held. It wasn't until July 3, 2014, that officials confirmed what many had suspected—the remains indeed belonged to the Jamisons.

Despite this closure, the questions regarding their demise lingered. The state of the remains was such that no definitive cause of death could be determined, leaving the final chapter of the Jamison family's story unwritten. Instead, their fate became a haunting echo through the wilderness, leaving bystanders to ponder the mystery of what truly happened in those woods.

## Theories That Haunt the Case

Before the tragic discovery of their remains, several chilling possibilities surfaced about what might have happened to Bobby, Sherilynn, and their young daughter, Madyson.

### A Family Enshrouded in Mysteries

The Jamison family's story is wrought with allegations and bitter disputes. Bobby Jamison had embarked on a legal battle against his father, Bob Dean Jamison, alleging threats, violence, and murky involvement in criminal activities. The tension was palpable, as Bobby accused his father of attempting vehicular assault in November 2008 and warned of his father's dangerous connections to meth and illicit enterprise. Despite these grave accusations, authorities ultimately discounted Bob Dean as a suspect in the family's vanishing act.

## Dark Dealings and Eerie Behavior

In the aftermath of the Jamisons' disappearance, some conjectured that the family had entangled themselves in the illegal drug trade. Investigators were drawn to this theory by the substantial amount of cash discovered in their abandoned truck, coupled with the family's bizarre conduct before they vanished. Their pastor, Gary Brandon, recalled unsettling conversations where Bobby spoke of ghosts haunting their residence and even referenced The Satanic Bible.

## The Ghosts of Conspiracy

Another theory that refuses to fade is that the Jamison family fell victim to a cult. Sherilynn's mother, Connie Kokotan, asserted that a religious sect had marked them for death. This chilling hypothesis was fueled by an array of mysterious events, including anonymous calls from former cult members and peculiar graffiti found on property containers. Adding an unsettling twist, tales emerged of Sherilynn acquiring a "witch bible," although her friends claimed it was merely a joke.

### Missteps in the Wilderness

Amidst the swirling theories, there lies a more mundane possibility—the family simply succumbed to the elements. Their remains were discovered just 2.7 miles from their truck, raising the theory of them getting lost and perishing from exposure. However, questions linger about why seasoned adults would be so unprepared for the wilderness, leading some to doubt this straightforward explanation.

### Dark Family Tensions

The Jamison family's history of inner turmoil cannot be ignored. A letter discovered in their abandoned vehicle painted a portrait of discord, with Sherilynn expressing deep-seated resentment toward Bobby. This has led to speculation about a potential murder-suicide, though Sherilynn's mother staunchly insists that the couple would never have endangered Madyson.

### Drug-Related Entanglements

Though some rumors suggested possible drug involvement, concrete evidence remains elusive. Former sheriff Beauchamp entertained this possibility but found no definitive proof linking the family to drugs, leaving this theory as an open-ended question.

---

Despite myriad theories, the truth behind the Jamison family's disappearance remains frustratingly out of reach.

Each avenue explored seems to lead to a dead end, with the only certainty being the haunting absence of definitive closure. The Jamison case will forever echo with unanswered questions, standing as a grim reminder of the mysteries that linger just beyond the veil of what we know.

# CHAPTER SIXTEEN
## THE LEGEND OF THE SANDOWN CLOWN

In the final chapter of this true crime anthology, we depart from the path of traditional crime narratives and step into the unsettling yet alluring realm of the unexplained. Welcome to the legend of the Sandown Clown—a tale that blurs the line between reality and the paranormal, and one that has ensnared my curiosity in its eerie grasp.

Our story begins in May 1973, on the serene shores of Lake Common in Sandown, an unassuming town on the Isle of Wight in the UK. The scene is set with the innocent laughter of two children enjoying their holiday, unaware that they were about to encounter something that would defy explanation. Lured by the distant, haunting sound of a siren—a noise reminiscent of an ambulance—the children crossed a footbridge over a placid stream. And there, they were met with an unusual sight.

Standing before them was an entity so bizarre that it defied categorization, a strange amalgamation of clown, robot, and alien. Its appearance was nothing short of otherworldly, yet it exuded a peculiar warmth in its interactions with the children. Despite its apparent shyness, it engaged them in gentle conversation for nearly thirty minutes, leaving them both bewildered and oddly comforted.

The encounter ended as mysteriously as it had begun. The Sandown Clown vanished, leaving no trace behind, swallowed by the mists of mystery that had birthed it. It was never seen again, yet the legacy of that day has woven itself into the fabric of local folklore, whispered among those who dare to entertain the possibilities of the unknown.

I invite you to join me in pondering the enigma of the Sandown Clown—a tale not marked by crime but woven with the threads of intrigue and mystery. This haunting narrative beckons us to peer into the shadows where the known meets the unexplainable, and to consider the possibility that not all mysteries are meant to be solved.

---

Imagine, if you will, a figure nearly seven feet tall, imbued with a delicate, almost ethereal presence. This was Sam. While his stature was commanding, his form was slender, and his appearance straddled the line between human and alien. Standing in the woods, Sam possessed a human-like silhouette with two arms, two legs, and a perfectly round head that seemed oversized for his frame. His skin, white and paper-like, contrasted starkly against the natural surroundings, while his facial features appeared hastily sketched—a pair of blue triangles for eyes, a brown rectangle for a nose, and a thin oval mouth with yellow lips that remained motionless, even as he spoke or ate.

His attire only heightened his strangeness. Draped in a red and green clown-like suit, Sam sported a tall, pointed hat crowned with a bobble. He wore dark blue gloves, each with just three fingers. Wooden antennae jutted from his head, wrists, and ankles, blurring the line between costume and reality.

The first encounter with Sam began with an eerie siren, reminiscent of an ambulance, a sound so strange it drew the curiosity of two unsuspecting children. Fay, a seven-year-old girl, was enjoying a playful afternoon near a lake in Sandown, Isle of Wight, during May 1973 when she heard the unsettling noise. Intrigued, she and her friend followed the sound across a golf course and into the marshes near Sandown Airport. The sudden silence was broken by the sight of a blue-gloved hand with three fingers gripping a wooden footbridge.

From beneath the bridge emerged a towering figure who fumbled a book into the water. He moved toward a peculiar, windowless metallic hut that seemed to absorb him. Despite their apprehension, the children, driven by curiosity, decided to follow.

When they reached the hut, the figure reappeared, clutching a device that resembled a microphone. The siren blared again, louder than before. Through this contraption, Sam addressed them, his voice unexpectedly clear and soothing, "Hello, are you still there?" Encouraged by the calming tone, the children approached the being, who identified himself as Sam.

Standing before them, Sam was an odd sight indeed—nearly seven feet tall, neckless, and garbed in a green tunic with white pants and a yellow pointed hat. His face featured red hair, a brown square nose, and triangular eyes. Yet despite his bizarre appearance, Fay found Sam's demeanor kind and non-threatening. With a mix of speech and written notes, he communicated his identity, professing he was neither ghost nor man, but something beyond their understanding. He admitted his fear of humans, believing they might wish him harm.

The children accepted his invitation to explore his dwelling. Inside, they discovered a rudimentary yet otherworldly environment—a self-fashioned two-story hut. The metallic floors and blue-green patterned walls mirrored Sam's enigmatic presence. Wooden furniture, simplistic in design, filled the space, where a small electric heater struggled to warm the air.

The most astonishing demonstration came when Sam showed them how he consumed berries. He would thrust his head forward, and in a bizarre display, the berries seemed to dance between his eyes before disappearing into his mouth, defying conventional biology.

When asked his name, Sam enigmatically responded, "I am all colors." The encounter left the children bewildered, filled with more questions than answers, pondering the existence of this strange, otherworldly visitor in their otherwise ordinary lives.

**A Lingering Mystery**

In the chapters of unexplained phenomena, the tale of Sam the Sandown Clown stands out as one of the most elusive mysteries. It all began with a meeting that seemed to defy the boundaries of reality itself. Sam vanished as mysteriously as he appeared, leaving behind a solitary report filed by "Mr. Y," the young girl's father, with the British UFO Research Association (BUFORA). This account, retold by his daughter, "Target Fay," only deepened the intrigue surrounding the encounter. Was Sam a mere prankster, a mysterious human in disguise, an apparition from local folklore, or an entity far beyond our comprehension?

For thirty minutes, Fay and her companion engaged in a surreal exchange with Sam, before fear drove them back to familiar ground. It was clear that the experience had left an indelible mark. Three weeks after meeting the entity, Fay and her friend still resolved to keep Sam's existence a secret from the world.

That decision changed on June 2, 1973, when Fay's father noticed her unease. Initially dismissive of his daughter's outlandish story, Mr. Y's skepticism was eroded by the detailed account she provided. Wanting to validate the story, he turned to the young boy, who confirmed the meeting but remained reluctant to discuss it further.

Compelled by an unsettling intuition, Mr. Y contacted a BUFORA investigator and submitted a comprehensive report. Mr. Y's interest in UFOs was not merely academic; he had his own history of strange encounters. Back on October 20, 1970, he witnessed a large, silent UFO with seven vivid lights hovering over fields near Brading. This anomaly pursued him, often appearing in his rearview mirror. Over the next two years, these sightings recurred, culminating in a chilling incident at Compton Bay, where he observed yellow lights in the water.

Mr. Y suspected a link between Fay's encounter with Sam and his own experiences. He speculated that Fay had been drawn into an "alien reality," especially since two nearby golf course workers that day appeared oblivious to Sam's presence. Though he wished for the story to be taken seriously, he hesitated to share it widely, fearing ridicule and disbelief.

The Sandown Clown case remains one of the most perplexing "UFO" stories, marked by its supernatural elements and the curious nature of Sam—a being that seemingly blurred the lines between alien, clown, and ghost. The interaction between Sam and Fay, whether through alien intent or otherworldly mischief, continues to baffle and intrigue.

Theories abound. Was Sam an elaborate hoax, a human trickster or potential predator in disguise, or a visitor from another dimension? Some ponder supernatural origins, while others consider the possibility of a shared hallucination. Yet, despite the lack of resolution, the legend of Sam the Sandown Clown persists, woven into local folklore. It enthralls us with its mix of whimsy and mystery, challenging us to reconsider the frontiers of our reality and the secrets that lurk in its shadows.

Did the children invent the tale? Did Mr. Y orchestrate a grand hoax and force the children to be complicit in that? Or could the Sandown Clown have been a malevolent figure, sparing these two by mere chance? Why has no one seen him again? The questions remain tantalizingly unanswered, continuing to captivate and unsettle those who dare to peer into the obscure corridors of this mystery.

---

Continue with True Crime Sleep Stories: Volume 3
Available on Amazon

# AFTERWORD

And so, we draw the curtains on another sinister voyage with *True Crime Sleep Stories, Volume 2*. I can't thank you enough for joining me on this spine-tingling ride. Your unyielding support remains the heartbeat that drives these tales. I hope *Volume 2* has stirred your curiosity about the darker corners of the human mind as much as *Volume 1* did. These stories remind us that the most intriguing mysteries often lurk in the shadows just beyond our sight. Until we meet again, sleep with one eye open, keep your head on a swivel, and lock those doors tight. Who knows what hidden secrets might be lurking just outside your window? Thank you for stepping into the darkness with me—it's been quite an adventure!

- Kelli Brink

---

Continue with True Crime Sleep Stories: Volume 3
Available on Amazon

# ABOUT THE AUTHOR

Kelli Brink has spent several years at the forefront of podcasting, seamlessly blending her roles as a host and consultant to create compelling narratives. A graduate of the University of Iowa with a Bachelor's degree in Communication Studies, Kelli's passion for storytelling traces back to her childhood when she transformed everyday objects into imaginary microphones. With an early love for radio, music, and all things audio, she has honed her craft to captivate audiences.

When she's not behind the microphone or advising clients, Kelli loves to explore new cities, camp, kayak, attend live music shows, or enjoy a cold beverage around a campfire with friends and family. Now, she brings her talents to the world of true crime, offering readers a deep, gripping look into the darker sides of human nature.

instagram.com/truecrimesleepstories

youtube.com/@TrueCrimeSleepStoriesPodcast

www.ingramcontent.com/pod-product-compliance
Lightning Source LLC
Chambersburg PA
CBHW022333280326
41934CB00006B/615

*9798892341264*